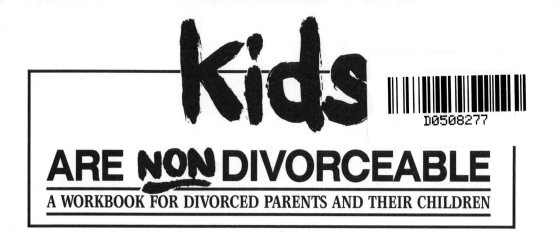

Kids
ARE NON DIVORCEABLE

A WORKBOOK FOR DIVORCED PARENTS AND THEIR CHILDREN

AGES 6-11 VERSION

SARA BONKOWSKI, Ph.D.

ACTA Publications
Chicago, Illinois

KIDS ARE NONDIVORCEABLE
A Workbook for Divorced Parents
and Their Children
Ages 6-11 Version

BY SARA BONKOWSKI, Ph.D.

Dr. Bonkowski is Associate Professor of Social
Work at Aurora University in Aurora, Illinois
and the founder of the Myrtle Burks Center
for Clinical Social Work in Glen Ellyn, Illinois.

Edited by Gregory F. Augustine Pierce
Design by Hirt and Associates
Artwork by Isz

Copyright © 1987   ACTA Publications
4848 N. Clark Street
Chicago, Illinois 60640
(312) 271-1030

Library of Congress Catalogue No. 87-071988
ISBN No. 0-915388-31-6
Printed in the United States of America

CONTENTS

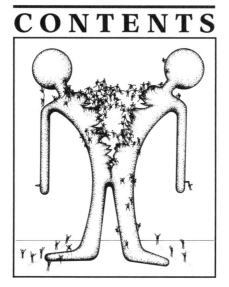

**TO MY PARENTS,
SARA ELIZABETH MCDONALD EDGELL
AND
GEORGE PAUL EDGELL,
WHO TAUGHT ME ABOUT PARENTING AND FAMILIES.**

ACKNOWLEDGMENTS

This book became a reality with the vision and help of others. Mary Buckley had a sensitivity to the needs of divorced parents and children and wanted to provide them with a helpful resource. John Nolan gave me the encouragement I needed to write. He has mastered much of the current divorce literature, and this made our conversations stimulating. Judith Bertacchi and Gerard Weber read the manuscript thoroughly, providing helpful suggestions—many of which were incorporated. The crucial, final organization and editing of the text was done by Gregory Augustine Pierce. His sense of structure and detail helped in completing the book.

This is a book about families, and my family helped in every phase of the writing process. My husband, John Mulherin—who is a busy lawyer—typed the entire manuscript into the word processor. My son, Brian Bonkowski, served as "editor-in-residence," and my step-daughter, Kim Mulherin, not only helped with the word processing but provided valuable feedback from her perspective—the perspective of a child whose parents are divorced. Karla Bonkowski, my daughter, and Kelly Mulherin, my other step-daughter, contributed by being active adolescents, forcing all of us to think about something other than writing this book.

Finally, I want to acknowledge all the divorcing parents and their children who have shared their struggles and growth with me.

CHAPTER 1

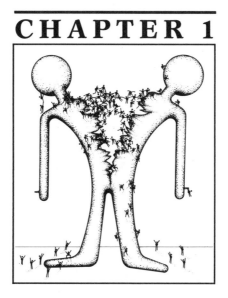

BEGINNING TO REBUILD

*"I really don't want my parents to get back together . . .
When I look back on it, I can see our family wasn't that
happy. I didn't know it at the time, but I do now. Do you
understand what I mean?"*

Steven, an eleven year old boy.

Steven is an exceptionally bright, talented, outgoing child, but when his
parents, Tony and Joan, separated and then divorced, his world almost fell apart.
Both of his parents experienced depression and the family lost their home because
of financial problems. Steven's grades plummeted and he began getting bad conduct reports from his teachers.

Steven and his family—his mother, father and sister Margaret—worked together very hard to understand and accept the divorce and the many changes it
had caused in their lives. They even attended family counseling sessions for over
fourteen months. Steven's grades have now begun to improve and Joan has managed to find a comfortable townhome for herself and the children near their
school. Steven and Margaret spend many weekends with Tony, and the parents—
despite their divorce—have continued the process of "co-parenting" their children.

This progress happened only because Steven's parents made a commitment to
help their children deal with their divorce. Despite the embarrassment and pain
it caused them, they talked with Steven, Margaret, with each other, and with the

counselor about the divorce. As a result, this family is beginning to heal and rebuild their lives.

When parents divorce, they may find themselves in the position of Steven's parents: caught up in their own emotional, financial and legal struggles, but recognizing that their children are struggling too. *All* children are in some way affected by the divorce of their parents. Even those children who show no observable signs of stress due to their parents divorce are sure to react in some way at some time. On the other hand, not *all* problems of children of divorced parents are divorce-related. Children in families with two parents living together also have many difficulties. Identifying which issues in each child's development might be connected to the divorce and then dealing with those issues in a sensitive and mature manner is the special task of every divorced parent.

PRE-ADOLESCENT

No one age group seems to be more or less affected by divorce than another. There are, however, great differences in how children in different stages of their development understand and accept what has happened to their family. Recognizing developmental changes and offering suggestions to help children from infancy to young adulthood is difficult enough—without adding the special situations caused by divorce. Therefore, I have opted to narrow the focus of this workbook to children between the ages of six and eleven—what we call "pre-adolescence."

Grade school age children have many qualities in common. They are developing an ability to think abstractly and to reason, accumulating basic social skills, and increasing involvement with their peers. Even within this age group, however, there are considerable differences. One six year old may seem quite babyish and not even able to understand the concept of "divorce," while another six year old will be very concerned with the issues of child support payments and visitations. Some eleven year olds are really young adolescents, and should be understood through that lens, while others are still comfortable with being just a "kid." It is important for you to know and understand each of your children, and this understanding will form a basis for how you work with each child.

This workbook is designed to help you share experiences with your pre-adolescent children which will enable them to to accept and adjust to the reality of your divorce. This process will succeed to the extent that you focus on the individual needs of each child. I will use the words "child" and "children" interchangeably to take into account the many instances of more than one pre-adolescent in a family, but—whether there are one or many children—it is important that each be dealt with as a unique individual.

THE PROCESS OF ADJUSTING

Rebuilding a family after a divorce is not easy or pain free. Each family member has experienced many losses and now has major adjustments to make. In addition to the personal losses, family members often feel social stigma. Although divorce is no longer an unusual phenomenon, it still often carries negative connotations for those involved. The terms used in divorce—plaintiff, defendant, fees, alimony, custody, non-custodial parent—communicate a legalistic, objective system which certainly influences a divorcing family's future. How awful it feels to have these terms applied to oneself!

As you know, your family is not just a legal entity, but a very personal, unique structure. In writing about divorce, one cannot escape the use of legal terminology. Although these terms are related to your pain, the concepts have been designed by the judicial system and the legislature to protect you and your children. While it is important to look at legal realities such as visitation and custody issues in a human, caring manner, none the less the fact is that in divorce there are legal constraints and limits for each parent and the children.

The ideas and suggestions in the following chapters have been gathered from several sources. As a clinical social worker, I see divorcing families—children and parents—in family and individual therapy. I facilitate adjustment groups for divorcing adults. I also lead a Saturday morning group for school age children whose parents are separated or divorced. I have seen some families from the time they first begin to contemplate divorce and other families that came for help only after years of bitter post-divorce hostilities. Many of the case illustrations cited in this book are drawn from these clinical experiences. To preserve anonymity I have, of course, used fictitious names and have altered other identifying information relating to the children and families. Some of my (present and past) clients may think that they recognize their children or family situations, but I assure them that this is only because many factual divorce situations, conflicts, and struggles are remarkably similar.

In addition to my first hand experience in helping divorcing families, I study, teach college classes, and conduct research on aspects of the family and divorce. Finally, I am a parent, with two children, and I personally experienced divorce almost ten years ago. Some of my close friends have divorced, and we have shared with each other—as good friends do—our own reactions to divorce. I have observed my own children's and my friends' children's adjustment to divorce. This book is, therefore, an integration of clinical, scholarly and personal experience.

Divorce is often such a difficult trauma for all family members that children may feel that they are unable to contribute, grow and give. To regain a positive life outlook for your child, draw upon any source that is helpful . . . this book should be but one of your resources. Others may include your family, friends and religious faith.

THE EXERCISES

In using this book, you are to be the primary "helper" for your child. At the end of each chapter you will find exercises for you and exercises for your child or children. Most exercises for the parent are to be done a day or two (or even a week) before working with the child. Each parent exercise is very similar in format and was designed to help you sort out your ideas, feelings, and possible solutions related to each topic prior to working with your child. You will be more open to listening to your child after you yourself have faced the feelings and thoughts each topic raises. Thus, when working with your child you will be prepared to be a calm, sensitive, somewhat objective helper. The topics in the book are arranged in an order which will be most helpful in the rebuilding process:

- helping children understand why their parents divorced;
- assessing the changes the divorce created for each child developmentally;
- understanding how divorce makes a family different;
- looking at each child's reaction to the divorce;
- discussing the problems associated with visitations and other post-decree concerns;
- knowing how other significant people play a role in divorce adjustment;
- dealing with the difficult issues of parental dating and remarriage;
- and finally, projecting the future for each child and understanding how parental divorce continues to be an important influence throughout life.

Each topic tends to build on the proceeding one, so do the exercises in order. A child may not be emotionally ready to think about the future, for example, when he or she has not yet dealt with the past or present.

The abilities and interests of children between the ages of six and eleven will vary considerably. A young six year old will probably just be beginning to develop reading and writing skills, whereas by ten or eleven many children are able to write stories and read complex materials. Each of the exercises take into consideration children's ages and skill levels. At the end of most chapters are separate exercises that will be appropriate for younger grade school children (ages six through eight) and another designed for the older child (ages nine through eleven). Do not, however, hesitate to use an exercise designed for a younger child for an older one, or vice versa. You might also want to adapt a particular exercise to your specific needs, or invent an entirely new exercise on your own.

Do not force your children to do the exercises exactly as you have planned, or even to do them at all. Give children the opportunity to choose a time when dealing with the divorce is possible for them and when engaging in a creative project with you might be fun for them.

If you have more than one child between the ages of six and eleven, some of the children's exercises will be fun to do with everyone working together, while other exercises are best done alone allowing each individual child some private time and attention. If you do joint exercises however, be sure that you stress that each child may have different ideas about a particular subject. . .and that this is all right. The discussion of these different perspectives while working on the project may help enlarge each child's view of divorce.

A variation to working with just your own child might be to include a divorced friend's child to participate. This can be a way of beginning to expand your child's understanding and acceptance of divorce. This may also be a way to encourage a reluctant child to participate.

The exercises use materials most families have at home or are able to obtain easily and inexpensively: white paper (8 x 10 or 10 x 14), colored construction paper, color markers or crayons, chalk, poster paints (optional), scissors, pencils, paste, and old magazines and photos. Some exercises require no materials, only time to spend with your child.

Many of the exercises use some type of "projective" technique such as story telling or painting. In a projective experience, children will draw upon feelings and ideas of which they may not be fully conscious. Putting these ideas and feelings into a story or picture can be very healing and therapeutic. Just *doing* the exercises can help children experience and resolve conflicts. Please try not to "over talk" your children, or they may begin to dread doing the exercises. Of course, when a child wants to talk about ideas and feelings doing the project has stimulated, be ready to listen and share—it will help both the child and you.

Your children's exercises may reveal that they are feeling very sad or very angry. It is often difficult for a parent to hear these powerful feelings, for they do not want their child to be in pain. To help your child feel better you may be tempted to say, "Oh it isn't that bad," or, "You really don't hate Daddy (or Mommy)." Please don't. If you discount your child's feelings or give a message that only happy feelings are acceptable, you will not help them deal with your divorce. Working on the exercises can be one way for your child to ventilate feelings which might otherwise be suppressed.

All people have a right to their own thoughts, feelings and ideas. Your child's reactions to your divorce may be somewhat different than yours. Remember you are not necessarily right and your child wrong. Each person has his or her own perspective, and your child necessarily has a child's perspective. It is not your task to get your children to "sing the company song," that is, agree perfectly with you.

Each child will view the divorce from his or her individual points of view. You, of course, see the divorce events from your perspective. *Both of you are "right" and neither of you is "wrong."*

Your task in helping your children is to allow them the freedom to express their own feelings and ideas, while being willing and able to give accurate, factual information when they need or want it. This will not always be an easy task, but your care for your child will make it possible.

When planning to do an exercise, be sure to pick a time that feels pressure-free (as much as that is ever possible for a single parent), and have the recommended supplies on hand. Despite careful timing and preparation, some children may be resistant to doing the exercises. If one child has this reaction, do not push him or her. The time may not be right to share feelings about the divorce with you. In this case, proceed through the book doing the exercises with other children or only those designed for the parent. Later on, perhaps in several months, you may once again try to do some of the exercises with that child. If your child never will do the exercises, understand that this may mean your child doesn't feel emotionally free to deal with the divorce with you. Perhaps he or she would talk to a friend or relative, a professional counselor outside the family, or—as much as you might hate to admit it—only with your former spouse.

Your other children might love to do the exercises and will look forward to your special time together. At times a child may like the exercises and at other times appear resistive. This is a very natural occurrence.

The use of the exercises suggested in this book may stretch out over six to nine months, whereas other parents and children may complete all of the exercises in several weeks. If your child resists doing the exercises try to assess whether he or she is defending against looking at the divorce issues or whether he or she just prefers doing something else at that time. Both are good reasons not to do the exercise then, but the two underlying reasons for not wanting to do the exercises mean very different things. A defense against looking at divorce issues means *"go slowly, do not push;"* a desire to do something else at that time means, *"try me tomorrow."*

Another word of caution about doing the exercises with your child. At the time of a divorce many children have found that their parents are not safe people to talk to. They find that if they express their honest ideas and feelings about the divorce, these may be expressions the parents do not want to hear. Parents may try to change a child's feelings to be more like their's, or a parent's ideas and feelings may be so intense that a child feels overwhelmed and decides it is not safe to be honest with this parent.

This may create a dilemma for you. When doing the exercises with your child, how honest and expressive will you be about your own feelings? It is always important to be honest with your child, but it is not necessary to tell your child all your feelings and thoughts on each issue. If a child shares with you how angry he or she feels toward you for filing for the divorce, try to accept that it is important for him or her to express that feeling. Think how *you* might have felt if your mother or father had filed for divorce! As good as it might feel to have your child console and support you, this is too big of an emotional task for a six to eleven year old child. As time goes on, and your children learn more about the divorce issues, they may come to accept and understand why you filed for divorce. They then may no longer feel so angry at you, but continue to feel sad about the loss of the family.

WHICH PARENT?

Either parent—mother, father; custodial, non-custodial—or both can benefit from reading this book and doing the exercises with their children.

If you only have your children with you twice a month you might want to try an exercise every other visit. The time your children spend with you is special. If you or your child feel pressured to get through the book, it may destroy the natural flow to healing. The exercises may begin to feel more like work than fun. On the other hand, if one weekend is especially rainy, and you find yourself with nothing to do, perhaps your child will be open and excited about doing two exercises.

Perhaps you are one of those lucky divorced parents that has an open, non-hostile relationship with the other parent. If this is the case, you may want to tell your former spouse that you are reading this book and doing the exercises with your children. This would give that parent a chance to read and think about the same ideas. I strongly recommend, however, that children *do not do* the exercises at both homes. This puts far too much pressure on them. If your former spouse is working with your children from this book, allow him or her this privilege—at least for the sake of the children! The worst thing for them would be for their parents to fight over who does the exercises with them. There are suggestions in the book about how two parents can cooperate with the children's exercises.

On the other hand, you and your former spouse may have a cool or hostile relationship. If you are in this situation, do not suggest the book to your former spouse. This does not mean "Keep it a secret from Dad (or Mom)." It means allow your former spouse the freedom to adjust to the divorce in his or her own way. Your suggestions regarding the children, although designed to help them, may be viewed as an intrusion or interpreted as an order. Do not use this book as another weapon in the marriage wars, but rather as an aid in healing and rebuilding both yourself and—especially—your children

A WORD OF CAUTION

Medicine, which can be very helpful and life saving, often also carries with it warnings about its misuse. In such a vein, there are two important concerns which must be raised before you begin.

The exercises you do with your children must *never* be used against your former spouse—*especially* not as ammunition in conflicting legal issues such as custody or visitation. What the children share with you in an open, trusting moment must *never* be used against the other parent. Even if it would give you great delight to tell your former spouse, "The children really hate your new girlfriend (or boyfriend) and don't even want to come visit your new apartment," Don't do it! The exercises were designed to help parents and children rebuild, not as a way to get revenge. If you do use the information gained in the exercises against your child's other parent it will damage your own relationship with your child by seriously destroying trust.

Secondly, you will discover that throughout the book parents are encouraged to work toward developing a healthy co-parenting relationship for the good of their children. In some instances this is impossible. There are a few parents who, for a number of complex reasons, are unable or unwilling to co-parent. There are even some parents that cannot parent. Occasionally, after a divorce one parent totally disappears from his or her child's life.

If your former spouse shows little or no interest in parenting, you may feel very hurt or angry. Or perhaps you are even happy to have him or her out of your life completely. Regardless of how you feel, however, try not to degrade your former spouse to your children; this type of behavior usually backfires. Generally, the more one parent puts down the other, the more the children dislike the complaining, hostile parent. Children do not like *anyone* talking about either parent in a negative manner. Children want to love both parents, even a parent who has apparently abandoned them. They feel sad and angry enough over the divorce and need help in understanding the new reality—not your feelings to add to theirs.

This does not mean that you have to be a cheerleader for someone you no longer like or respect. Don't be artificial with your children. Try to be somewhat objective in commenting about your former spouse, and allow the children to express their own feelings of sadness and disappointment without adding hostile comments and opinions. In time—with your help, the help of others (hopefully including your former spouse), and perseverance and prayer—your child will come to an emotional acceptance of the divorce and some relationship with or at least connection to both parents.

BEGINNING TO REBUILD

Use this book to understand yourself, your divorce experience, and your child. Recognize that these three elements are tied together. Remember, the adjustment process will take a considerable period of time. The essential fact to keep in mind is that the path of adjustment is never steady and that you may have to work on it over and over. On the other hand, by the time you finish this book, you may be surprised at how much progress you and your child or children have made.

14

EXERCISE 1

Putting the Pieces Back Together

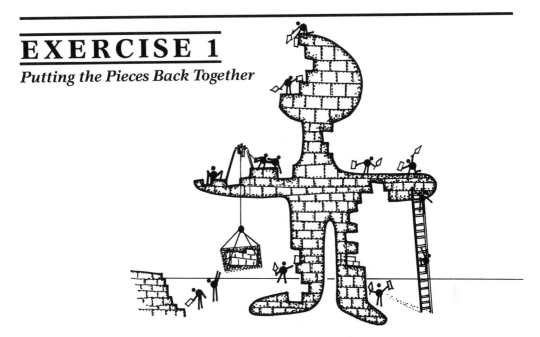

FOR BOTH PARENT AND CHILD

You will need a sheet of paper for each family member and some magic markers. Write each person's name at the top of one piece of paper. Then have each person write *one* word that best describes the past six months. If you have a young six or seven year old you may need to help with spelling or ideas. To make this exercise more fun you might use different color markers.

After everyone has written the first word put the papers on the refrigerator door or tape them to a sturdy wall. (Make sure the ink doesn't come through the paper, or you may have another joint project when you're finished!) Every day for a week have each person add one more word to his or her personal list. After seven days, each family member will have seven words describing the past six months.

(ONE FAMILY'S EXAMPLE)

JOE (FATHER, 35)	TIM (SON, 9)	SHERRY (DAUGHTER, 7)
Hectic	Different	Moving
Busy	Tiring	Awful
Frustrating	Sad	Sad
Sad	New friends	(Couldn't think of a word)
Angry	O.K.	Mad
Broke	Alone	Baby sitter
Fun	Busy	Fun

15

(COMMENT)

Joe is a divorced father with custody of two children. His first three words described activity, the middle two were feelings, the next word was about his financial position, and—finally—Joe remembered that in the past six months there were fun times. These words paint a fairly clear picture of the last six months for Joe: many changes and responsibilities, more expenses, sadness and anger, but also positive changes and fun.

Tim and Sherry needed some help thinking of words and sometimes they would copy a word from their Dad or each other. Tim, however, was the first one to mention a feeling—sad—and then both Sherry and Joe acknowledged that they felt sad too. One day Sherry just couldn't think of a word.

If your children copy your feelings or ideas, or cannot think of a word, do not push them. You may find it somewhat difficult for you, an adult, to think of seven words. You can imagine that a child may not always be able to come up with a new idea.

After a week of making your list, what have you learned about yourself and your children? How do the lists differ? Does each family member have a slightly different perception, or are most of your views and feelings quite similar?

When you have finished this project start a folder for each person. Place the folders in a safe place, but in a place where the children may look at their exercises whenever they want. These folders will accumulate some of your "divorce" work. It will be interesting for you to review all of your completed projects about six months after you have completed this workbook. By reviewing the projects, you can assess the process and progress of rebuilding for both your children and yourself.

CHAPTER 2

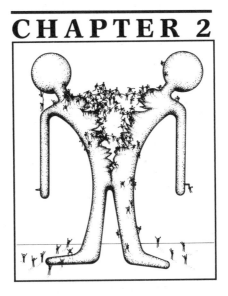

EXPLAINING YOUR DIVORCE TO YOUR CHILDREN

"My parents got divorced because they always got into fights"

Allen, an eight year old boy.

"I don't know why my parents got divorced"

Elizabeth, a ten year old girl.

Children need and want to know why their parents divorced. As they begin to understand, most children become more accepting of the drastic changes in their lives.

In many families, however, children have been provided with very little information about the divorce. Some parents assume that their children know the "whys" as well as they do themselves. After all, the parents assume, each child has been a part of the family and has experienced many of the same events as the parents. Other parents want to protect their children from experiencing or even knowing about unhappy or unpleasant events and therefore decide to tell them very little about the actual reasons for the divorce. Still other parents find the divorce to be so traumatic that it is difficult for them to talk to their children about it at all.

On the other hand, parents sometimes tell their children too much about the causes of their divorce. Often when a parent is very hurt and desperately needs a confidant, he or she will turn to a child as one would to an adult friend. One eleven year old girl remembers her mother getting her up in the middle of the night and driving with her through the city trying to catch her father with his girl friend. This same girl was forced to call various taverns and women's homes in search of her father. Although this example may appear extreme, it is not uncommon for a very isolated parent to over-involve a child.

Neither extreme—"Don't tell the children anything" nor "Get your children on your side"—is what the *children need*.

GUIDELINES

There are a few basic rules for discussing your divorce with your children:

1. Tell each child what he or she can understand for his or her age and maturity.

The ability to intellectually and emotionally understand certain aspects of your divorce will differ for your child at different ages. Most four year olds can barely understand the concept of divorce; if they even know the word they simply think it means "Daddy and Mommy don't live together." By the time children are six or seven, they may realize that lawyers and courts are involved and that divorce has meant a lot of changes for the family. By age eleven or twelve, children are very interested in how custody is decided. Older school age children have developed a sense of fairness, and they may want to be sure visitations and custody are equitable.

2. Always tell your child the truth.

When your child asks you something about the divorce always answer as honestly and completely as possible, taking into consideration what the particular child can absorb. Fabrications will be discovered sooner or later, and they will only confuse your child about the real reasons for the divorce. Dishonesty about the divorce will also cause your child to doubt your other statements.

3. Do not wait for your child to ask questions, take some initiative.

Children are often reticent about bringing up divorce-related issues or questions. This does not mean they have no questions, or don't want more information. It may mean they are taking their cues from you. If you are open, not blaming, and calm in your discussions about the divorce, then pertinent facts, feelings, and information will be shared naturally.

4. Do not use your child as an emotional confidant.

Sharing the facts and feelings a child needs to know to be able to accept the divorce is not the same thing as discussing everything related to the divorce about which you may have a need to talk. When people divorce, they usually need to go over and over the numerous small events that lead up to the divorce and to share with someone all of the details of the divorce process. Don't make your children bear this burden. They have enough to deal with already.

DIFFICULT SITUATIONS

Some of the reasons that couples divorce are almost incomprehensible to pre-adolescent children. Certain situations—including physically or psychologically unhealthy behavior—need to be carefully and lovingly explained to a child in language that he or she can understand.

Stephanie's husband Russ, for example, had been physically abusive to her for several years. Finally deciding that Russ would never change his violent behavior, she left with the children and filed for divorce. Stephanie told her six year old son, Sammy, "Daddy gets too angry, and sometimes when he is angry he hits Mommy. Mommy doesn't want to be hurt so she is not going to be married to Daddy anymore. You will get to see Daddy, and you don't need to be afraid of him because he loves you and won't hurt you." Stephanie explained the facts very simply. Although her young son had only witnessed one incident of violence, Stephanie felt that it was best to be honest about why she had decided to divorce her husband—yet she was careful not to make Sammy frightened of his father.

Stephanie told her eight year old daughter, Jennifer, "I know you have heard Daddy and me fighting. Sometimes when Daddy gets mad at me he cannot control himself and he hits me. Although he usually feels sorry the next day, it seems he hasn't been able to stop acting this way. I just can't be hurt again, so I am going to get a divorce from Daddy. That is why we moved into this apartment. You and Sammy will get to see Daddy often. You know Daddy has never hurt you so there is of course no reason to be afraid of him." Stephanie provided her daughter a few more details than her son about the causes of the divorce, again handling it in a manner which was truthful and reassuring.

An eleven or twelve year old child might have been told more about abusive personalities and whatever steps both parents had taken in an attempt to correct the problem.

Stephanie may have needed to share with someone all the details of how her husband beat her, her final decision to leave, and the complicated legal proceedings that were currently under way. If she gave in to the temptation to share these events with her children, however, it is possible that they would have become so emotionally enmeshed in the parental problems that they would have begun to fail in school, become emotionally depressed or started acting overly agitated. As it was, Sammy and Jennifer developed a good relationship with their father, and they never experienced even the threat of physical abuse from him.

Unpleasant events have almost always preceded the decision to divorce. Sometimes these events or behaviors have had a severely negative impact on children. In these situations it is necessary to help a child work through the facts on a level that he or she can emotionally master.

If you were involved, for example, in a love affair before the end of your marriage, your child might ask, "Did Ben cause you and Daddy to get divorced?" You could answer something like this: "I knew Ben and even loved him before Daddy and I were divorced, so in some ways knowing Ben probably was one reason we got divorced when we did. But you should know that I was not in love with Daddy for two or three years before I even met Ben. Do you want to talk about what caused me to stop loving Daddy?"

Notice in this example that the details of the love affair are not discussed. The child did not ask for the details. Do not give children more than they want to know.

Conversely, do not use a child's age to avoid unpleasant facts. One mother told her six and seven year old girls that she would tell them why she and their father divorced when they were sixteen! Meanwhile, these girls could conjure up all sorts of awful reasons why the parents divorced. Imaginations often paint worse pictures than the truth. In this situation, the father—a college professor—had fallen in love with one of his older students. A six or seven year old could have understood: "Daddy fell in love with someone else, and it made Mommy very sad and angry." This would be much easier to understand and accept than the promise of revealing some mysterious secret in nine or ten years.

WHY DO PARENTS DIVORCE?

Children need to know that they did not cause their parents' divorce and that the causes of divorce are adults' problems—not theirs.

To effectively explain your divorce to your children, you must understand the reasons for it yourself. It takes months or years of serious deliberation and unhappiness before most couples decide to divorce, and even then the reasons are not always clear even to themselves.

Sometimes either the husband or the wife decides that the unhappiness or pain that he or she is experiencing in the marriage is worse than the pain and changes the divorce will bring on everyone involved. It becomes obvious to him or her that divorce is the only solution. It is not always so understandable to the other spouse—or to the couple's children.

Sometimes the decision to divorce is mutual. Both spouses decide the marriage is not working and they come to a divorce settlement amicably. They and their children begin to rebuild a different life, keeping disruptions to a minimum. Such divorces are rare, and even so the children will experience losses and change.

Most divorces are the result of a complicated process between two people. Each divorce is unique, just as each marriage is unique. It is impossible to list all the reasons why marriages which start out with so much promise end with so much pain. There are, however, several main causes of divorce in the United States...some of which are interrelated. It is the inability of a couple to communicate, compromise or change on these issues which finally results in the decision that they can no longer remain married. Here are ten of the basic causes of divorce, with some comments on how each effects children:

1. Personality Differences.

All people differ from each other psychologically. They have different personalities. Some people like things very neat and organized and become upset and even angry if anything is out of place. Other people are relaxed and productive in a messy home or office. Some are energetic in the morning, and others like to stay up late and really begin to come alive about ten or eleven at night. Some people need to share the details of daily living with others, while others may not like to talk very much. There are people who like cold climates, others hot. There are those who like to socialize with groups, while others prefer solitary types of activities. Some people require a lot of approval and praise, and some do not seem to care what others think.

These kinds of differences make us unique and interesting to each other. Your personality was formed by the interaction of many influences: where you lived growing up, how your parents related to you and to each other, your health, your own biological make up, how friends and teachers related to you and how you related to them, and whether you had brothers and sisters. These are just a few of the factors that influenced the formation of your personality. When you married, you assumed that your spouse was someone you could live with comfortably for the rest of your life.

When you live with someone intimately for a long time, however, you really begin to know his or her personality. As your mate's personality became known, perhaps you discovered differences that began to bother you. At first these differences may have appeared to be little annoyances. As time went on, however, they may have become more and more troublesome, until you finally felt you could no longer live with your partner.

Some people—and your children may be among them—believe that such relatively minor concerns do not justify divorcing. Many have discovered, however, that personality and psychological compatibility is at the core of a close marital relationship. Your children might be capable of understanding this, if you take the time to work with them on it.

2. Value Differences.

Just as each person has a unique personality, everyone has developed a philosophical stance on life that reflects his or her individual values and beliefs. What a person values and believes is very influential in the way he or she chooses to live life.

One person may value security and frugality. For this person, saving money by using discount coupons or buying things "on sale," staying at the same job, and owning a home and sticking close to it may be very important. Another person may value spontaneity and fun. This person may enjoy taking exotic vacations, going out often and staying late, making "impulse" purchases and not wanting the responsibility of having children. A person may believe mankind is basically good; this person will be trusting and hopeful. Another may believe most people are basically "bad" and thus be suspicious and on-guard around others. When married people discover that some of their fundamental values or beliefs are not shared by their partners, disagreements and arguments may begin to fester.

Money issues are frequently cited as a reason for divorce. Couples fight about not having enough money or how money is to be spent. Below the surface of these recurring disagreements are usually opposing values not only about material possessions but also about work and social status.

Religious differences are often a cause of marital problems. Sometimes varied doctrines or customs are the direct cause of friction. More often, the difficulties are less a matter of denominational affiliation or practice as they are different levels of fervor and involvement in religious activity.

Child rearing itself is another area of strong values and beliefs. One spouse may believe, for example, that it is important to give a child wide exposure to extra-curricular activities, such as dancing, sports or scouts, while the other may feel that it is dangerous for a child to be over-involved in such activities. One may forbid dating before sixteen, the other may feel it is good for younger teens to have boyfriends or girlfriends. One may be pro-allowance, another opposed to giving children money unless it is earned.

It is very difficult to change someone's values. No one changes them as the result of an argument with a spouse. People decide to get divorced because they learn over time that their ideas on a wide variety of matters are significantly different from those of their spouse and because they can find no mutually acceptable way to reconcile or respectfully accept these differences. Children are often caught in this conflict both before and after the divorce. They can understand these differences, however, without being forced to side with either parent.

3. Another Person.

Many marriages end in divorce when one of the partners falls in love with another person. When this happens the partner who has been left usually feels devastated. The parent with the new relationship will want the children to know and like his or her new love partner, and the "new couple" may want to include the children in activities. The other "dumped" parent often feels rage and contempt for the third party and try to recruit the children on his or her side.

When one partner falls in love with someone else, it is usually because there were already considerable personality and value differences in the marriage. For at least one spouse, the relationship was already dead. Children can learn to accept this, even if it is difficult for them to understand at their age. What they do not need is for one parent to use them as a weapon to punish the other. As comforting as this may seem ("I have an ally against my former spouse"), it is emotionally very bad for a child.

4. Excessive Drinking and Abuse of Drugs.

Substance abuse is a disease that touches many families. This illness may contribute to the events leading up to the divorce. Excessive drinking or drug use often result in violence, automobile accidents, loss of employment and physical illness. There are, however, many substance abusers who do not miss work and are never violent, yet their drinking or drug consumption does numb their feelings. They remove themselves emotionally from the family, being unavailable as a companion, friend, parent, or lover. Children almost always see the results of this disease, even if they do not realize the causes. With help, they can understand it as a reason for divorce.

5. Physical, Sexual or Emotional Abuse.

There are people who have low self-esteem, are quick to anger and easily frustrated. In a marriage, these people can become abusive to their mates and/or children. In many cases, this tendency can be traced to their own childhood experience of abuse or neglect. Regardless of the reason a person is abusive, it is always damaging for both the other spouse and the children to remain in such a situation.

The most common type of abuse occurs when men—who are stronger and have been given cultural messages of superiority—abuse a woman. There are women, however, who have been excessively cruel and abusive to their passive husbands. Another tragic pattern is when one or both parents are abusive to their children.

If you or your child were abused during your marriage, it is important for the children to be able to discuss the fear and anger they felt at those times and also to share the sense of sadness and relief when the family finally separated to become safe. Many children who have been abused need and greatly benefit from professional counseling.

6. Career Conflict.

Excessive career demands on one or both partners or conflicting career choices sometimes place stress on the marital relationship. Sometimes one spouse or the other will put all of his or her energy into the job, leaving little for the family. In the extreme, this can become the disease of "workaholism." The need to move with a job—especially from city to city—or to travel extensively can add to the pressures on a marriage.

Special problems caused by the need for day care can add to these conflicts, and children sometimes come to the conclusion that they are causing the marital conflict by the very fact of their existence.

7. Financial Pressures.

Decline or loss of family income or assets may prove to be too much pressure for the marriage to endure. The loss of money does not in and of itself cause the divorce. It is rather the stress caused by constant confrontation by bill collectors, bankruptcy, or the loss of the family home or business which can result in a loss of self-esteem and increased family instability.

Children also experience this financial pressure and again can be made to feel that they are partly to blame for the family's financial problems and therefore for their parents' divorce.

8. Homosexuality or Bisexuality.

People with homosexual or bisexual leanings sometimes marry and even have children. As the years pass, these people may experience the stress of not being able to express their true sexual longings. Sometimes the desire to be more honest about their sexual preference results in the termination of their marriage. Knowing of a parent's homosexuality or bisexuality may cause special adjustment problems for school age children.

9. Immaturity.

Some couples marry young—before their adult personalities have formed and before they have had an opportunity to experience a variety of social experiences. These people were simply not mature enough to make the lifelong commitment of marriage. It often happens that one partner may grow emotionally or intellectually while the other remains basically the same as when they were married. At about the age of thirty, or thirty-five, one or both of the partners may simply feel bored or tired of the marriage and want to get out to have new, fresh experiences. To family, friends, and even their children, this may not appear to be a good reason to divorce. Yet for the person, the prospect of living forty more years with a partner in a deadened relationship seems untenable.

10. Mental Illness.

When one partner has a serious mental illness, such as schizophrenia, the other partner may decide to divorce so that he or she can build a life with more stability. In these situations the healthy spouse may feel guilty deserting a mentally ill person, and the children might even blame that spouse for being unfaithful. It may, however, be the only step possible to create an acceptable environment for the healthy spouse and the couple's children.

* * *

Children can understand to some degree all of the above reasons for their parents' divorce. What is most important is that the reasons be presented to each child individually and geared to the child's age and maturity. Explanations should be done in an honest manner yet without giving the child details he or she neither requests nor can handle. This takes some initiative and skill on the part of the parent.

If both you and your former spouse basically see the reasons for the divorce in the same way, your children will be receiving similar messages from each of you about the reasons for the divorce. If you each see the deterioration process of your marriage very differently, your child will, of course, be receiving conflicting messages. Your child may even conclude that one of you is lying, when actually both of you are basically telling the truth from your own perspective. In that case, your children may need extra help in making sense of why two people they trust and love think so differently.

* * *

EXERCISE 2
The Many "Whys" of Divorce

FOR YOU

Take a piece of paper, and across the top write "Why We Divorced." Along the side of the paper write your name and your former spouse's name. Using the categories described in this chapter, write down what you think each of you would perceive as the major factors contributing to the divorce, listing them in order of importance. Of course, you cannot be sure of exactly how your former spouse perceives the causes of the divorce, but since the two of you have dealt with each other extensively concerning divorce issues you should have a good idea about his or her perceptions. After citing what you and your former spouse think are the major factors leading to the divorce, see what—if any—are major differences between your perceptions. If there are differences that may be continuing to cause conflicts/tension write down any ideas you might have about how you can make the post-divorce atmosphere and adjustment easier for your child.

(BILL'S EXAMPLE)
WHY WE ARE DIVORCED

MY REASONS:

1. Value and Belief Differences.

I have an MBA and place great emphasis on education. Rita did not attend college, and has always devalued "book learning." Eventually this difference in our valuing of education became the focal point of arguments about the children. We don't even like the same kind of music.

2. We Married Too Early.

I married Rita before I had finished college. When I choose her I was really still a teenager.

3. Another Person.

After several unhappy, lonely years I met a woman, Marcia, who has many of my same interests. Eventually we fell in love. I would like to marry her.

MY FORMER WIFE'S (RITA'S) REASONS:

1. Another Person.

Rita feels that if it were not for Marcia we would still be together. She feels I was dishonest with her.

2. Value and Belief Differences.

Rita always thought that my family looked down on her and thought that they were too good for her. She feels that my family are high-brows and doesn't want our children to be raised with that snooty attitude.

IDEAS TO HELP OUR TEN YEAR OLD SON, EVAN

Obviously Rita and I see the process that lead to the divorce very differently, although we probably do agree that there were differences in the value we placed on education. We also agree that meeting Marcia had something to do with my finally leaving home.

To help Evan, I need to realize that Rita may never accept me being with Marcia, and that she will put Marcia down for sometime. I will do things with Evan and Marcia together only after more time has passed, and I will not take Marcia with me to pick Evan up at Rita's home.

I will try to answer any question Evan has about my feelings for Rita and/or Marcia. When he is older and has been in love himself, I will explain the process I experienced in falling out of love with his mother. I will try not to blame Rita (because Evan needs to love her), but by the time he is older I hope he will be able to accept and understand our differences.

(COMMENT)

Bill is a recently divorced father. As you can see from his comments, he realizes that there is nothing he can do about his former wife Rita's perceptions or feelings. He only has control over his own reactions to Rita, Marcia and Evan. For Evan's sake, Bill has decided to consider some of Rita's feelings. This will help take Marcia out of the limelight as a contributing factor to the divorce. Bill hopes that as Evan grows up he will be able to understand his parents' value differences and accept them both.

Bill has a limited understanding of how his former wife feels. If Rita had done this exercise, her perception of Bill and the divorce might be quite different. Bill sees himself and his actions from a positive point of view, but Rita—having been hurt and deceived—might very well see his actions more negatively. She might, for example, feel that she had fulfilled her original marital commitments by helping to put Bill through school, by keeping house and caring for Evan. She may feel that Bill had changed the rules halfway through the game.

In any case, doing this exercise helped Bill sort through the reasons for his divorce and prepared him to be more sensitive and responsive to his son's need to understand what had happened to his parents.

EXERCISE FOR AGES 6-8

You will need two hand puppets, one for you and one for your child. If he or she doesn't have puppets, you can make simple ones out of old white socks by drawing eyes and a mouth on the toe of each sock.

After you have your puppets ready you can "stage" a T.V. talk show where you interview your child, who is now Mr. Rabbit or Miss Bear. Ask him or her about why parents divorce. After the interview is complete, change roles and let your child be the host and interview you. You can include an idea or two your child hasn't mentioned.

When you have finished the puppet play you might continue discussing reasons parents divorce, suggesting that everyone (you, your former spouse, the child, his or her siblings) probably has different ideas about what has happened. The realization that there are many reasons for divorce and that not everybody sees a divorce in the same way are important lessons for a young child to learn.

Your child may have had so much fun with the puppets play that he or she will want to play it again; perhaps talking about non-divorce topics. You and your children have a new game!

EXERCISE FOR AGES 9-11

Have 8-10 pieces of paper and some sort of a paper binder or staples or brads. Also have markers or crayons, and sharp pencils.

Suggest that your child write a book entitled "Why Parents Divorce." To encourage your child to do this project, explain that by writing this book it may help him or her—and might even help other children—understand divorce.

Start with Chapter 1. Write across the top of a page: "Why Grownups Get Divorced." (You will write all of the chapter headings.) Under this heading your child can draw pictures or write words that tell why, in general, people might get divorced. There might be pictures of people fighting or money signs, or even the symbol for Women's Liberation. If your child has difficulty thinking of a reason you might share an example or two, situations that are different from your own.

For the next two chapters, ask your child to write why each of his or her parents thought the divorce happened. Some children may have difficulty envisioning that each parent might have different reasons, and this is where you might begin to help them understand.

Write Chapter 2: "*Mom Thinks* She and Dad Divorced Because..." This chapter may only have one sentence, picture or word.

Write Chapter 3: "*Dad Thinks* He and Mom Divorced Because..." This chapter also may only have one sentence, picture or word.

Finally, write Chapter 4: "*I Think* Mom and Dad Divorced Because..." This chapter gives your child permission to express his or her own ideas about the divorce. Allow the child to go on as long as he or she desires and to give as many different reasons as possible. If you disagree with some of the reasons the child lists, do not say that they are "wrong." Ask the child why he or she thinks they were a cause of the divorce and correct any factual errors, but allow the child to express himself without becoming defensive yourself.

After your child has finished the book, put it together in the binder or with staples or brads. Read the book together, and ask your child if he or she would like to share it with someone, perhaps even your former spouse. The process of making the book and talking about the causes of divorce will help your child to further understand your situation.

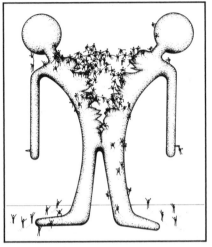

CHAPTER 3

DIVORCE MEANS MANY CHANGES

"Remember, Todd, your father will pick you up from school..."

Jeanne, a divorced mother.

"But, Mom, I wanted to play ball with Tommy...

Todd, her nine year old son.

Many changes affect all family members when parents divorce. Some of these changes create major losses: family home, a livable income, a shoulder to cry on. Other changes are so small that they might even go unrecognized: changes in routine, abandonment of a shared hobby, lack of help with the dishes or homework.

The stability which family roots provide is becoming increasingly important. Because of escalating social and technological changes, people need the physical, emotional, economic and spiritual anchor that a family can provide. Many members of divorcing families feel the loss of their family identity. Adults experience a vague, yet deep, sadness that comes from the disruption of family roots. Children wonder, "Am I an Anderson or a Caldwell?" Mom takes back her maiden name—often only to change it again if she remarries.

A fifth grader told that there will be a open house for parents experiences a pang in his stomach...his Dad just moved to Cleveland. A kindergartner now attends day care in the afternoon when she used to come home to eat lunch and play

31

with Mom...but now Mom must work full time. Dad goes home to an empty, silent apartment—no noise, no mess, no children. Mom wonders what to do with that "sick feeling" as the children disappear with Dad for the weekend. She's happy to have some free time, but she worries: will the children take a bath, will their father remember the cough medicine, will the children meet his new girlfriend?

Part of your responsibility as a parent is to deal with these changes yourself so that you can be helpful to your children in learning to adjust to the new situation.

BOTH PARENTS AS EMOTIONAL GUIDES

You are now engaged in rebuilding a family that consists of three interrelated parts: you and your children; your children and your former spouse; and you and your former spouse as co-parents. When a children are born, they are totally dependent upon others to see that they survive. As each year passes, a child will be able to do more and more things for himself or herself, until at some magical age between eighteen and twenty-one the child becomes a true adult. All children, however, even adult children, never outgrow the desire for parental concern and love.

Children of grade school age—between the ages of six and eleven—have already mastered many skills for living. They spend six or seven hours a day away from home at school, they can usually dress themselves, and can even clean their rooms and prepare simple meals. The pre-adolescent child looks to his or her parents to provide a secure, safe home base from which to venture out into the world. These children need to know that the parent and home will be there when needed. They want a person to cheer them up, help learn math problems, braid hair in the morning, fix a broken bike, take a splinter out of a finger, and laugh at a new "knock-knock" joke. They are counting on their parents to be there. A developing child in a real and special way needs the interest, help, concern, and love of both parents. . .a mother and a father. Divorce is especially difficult for these children.

When parents divorce, the child usually lives with one parent—referred to legally as the "custodial" parent. This parent has the legal right to make major decisions about the child. The other parent, the "non-custodial" parent, usually has visitation rights. These visitation patterns vary and may range from several visits with the children a week to one long stay in the summer. Many parents are able to work out a visitation schedule that feels equitable to them and is comfortable for the children.

In our society the mother has usually been granted custody of the children. Fathers are increasingly questioning this practice, asserting that they can perform the role of a primary, nurturing parent as well as the mother. In fact, some fathers have been named the custodial parent. Another variation is what is called "joint custody," with each parent having input into major decisions and the children spending blocks of time with each parent.

All of these custody arrangements create a major dilemma for grade school age children. These children have a great need for both parent's love, attention, interest and concern. When the divorce takes place one parent usually no longer has daily contact with the children, while the other parent has long periods of sole responsibility.

If you are the non-custodial parent, it may take dedication on your part to keep up contact with your pre-adolescent child. Some days he or she may not sound all that happy to talk to you. You son or daughter may not share little bits of news from school like in the "old days," and you may often get the feeling that he or she would rather be outside playing with neighborhood friends than talking with you. Your feelings are probably accurate. Yet such actions are not necessarily abnormal for any pre-adolescent nor aimed specifically at you. If you were still living with your child, many times he or she would run in, say "Hi, Dad," (or "Hi, Mom,") grab two cookies and be out the door. This is normal behavior for all six to eleven year olds. So when a child is comfortably engaged in his or her own world, a call from a non-custodial parent—no matter how missed or loved—is a distraction. In this situation, moreover, your call may be an intruding reminder that you no longer live there. This does not mean you shouldn't call—*you should* —for phone calls tell your child that you remember, you care. You are the adult parent meeting your child's needs...your child is not grown up enough to take care of you.

If you are the custodial parent, you need to reassure yourself that your child will be all right when away from you. It is often especially difficult for a mother— who, from the time a child was born, has been responsible for making most of the daily decisions about his or her welfare—to relinquish total control. You may worry that your child is not being cared for in the proper way. In most cases the non-custodial parent does in fact care for the child differently than the custodial parent would. But difference is neither wrong nor bad, it is just "different." If children occasionally sleep in a sleeping bag they are probably still safe and rested. If a child eats cheese sandwiches and raisins for breakfast this is almost as nutritional as traditional cereal and juice. Practice sending the children on visits with your former spouse with your blessing. Plan things for yourself to do while they are away so you won't worry as much.

Some custodial parents are so embittered because of the hurt experienced in the break up of the marriage that they do not want their children to have any contact with the non-custodial parent. This merely complicates things for the children. A cardinal axiom of parenting the children of a divorce is this: *children want to know and love both parents.* If you care for your children, try to put your own hurts aside and allow and even encourage them to know and continue to care for their other parent. When your children have grown they will thank you for understanding and permitting this open relationship.

Occasionally there is a parent who is so emotionally unstable that it might truly endanger a child to spend time alone with him or her. Parents who might fall into this dangerous category are chemically dependent people who drink or abuse drugs when children are around or parents who have been sexually, physically or emotionally abusive. If you suspect your former spouse fits one of these categories, discuss it with your attorney. Visitations may be arranged in a controlled environment. A note of caution: some parents hate their former spouse so much they unjustly accuse him or her of being abusive or chemically dependent in an attempt to control visitation. This type of vindictive behavior—even if supposedly meant to distance and perhaps protect your child—can easily backfire on you. It will only cause further damage to the child, and you run the risk of losing his or her respect and confidence.

YOUR CHILD'S AGE AND RESPONSE TO YOUR DIVORCE

Your child should be in grade school now. When you and your child have completed the exercises in this book (and other exercises you may create), it does not mean the subject of parental divorce has been dealt with and you can now forget about it. Children need to work and rework their parents' divorce. This process will continue throughout their lives. The understanding of a seven year old is very different from that of a twelve year old—which differs again from what is needed by an eighteen year old.

As children approach important developmental periods they often need to bring up aspects of the divorce again and again. For example, if your child was eight when you got divorced, he or she will probably need to spend some time rethinking the divorce at age eleven or twelve. This is the age when children are beginning puberty. They are dealing with issues of gender and future identity. Children of both sexes at this age want to know what went wrong in their parent's marriage. Children who have been living with one parent often contemplate changing custody at this age. They seem to long for the other parent. Such reconsideration of the divorce may take place again at sixteen, then again when a child leaves home, when he or she begins to contemplate marriage, and again around the time his or her own children are about the same age your child was when you divorced.

CHILDREN'S COPING MECHANISMS

Your child will often need to talk about the divorce in order to understand, accept, and mourn the loss of family. This may sound as if children are just waiting anxiously to pour out questions and feelings. Nothing could be further from the truth! Most children develop techniques to cope with all the changes. They develop and cling to a style that works for them, that saves them pain. Some common psychological terms used to describe methods of coping are "denial" (the divorce is not happening or the divorce is not sad), "repression" (I refuse to think about the divorce), "sublimation" (I will become so busy with swimming I won't have to deal with the divorce), or "projection" (this divorce is the fault of Dad's secretary; she's the villain). These coping processes are done subconsciously, so the child is usually unaware of how he or she copes.

Perhaps as you have been reading about these common coping mechanisms of children you may recognize ones you yourself use to help deal with difficult, painful problems. These psychological techniques are useful for a period of time until a person—child or adult—is strong enough to be able to carefully and slowly deal with problems. They should not continue forever, however. You as a parent can help your children come to grips with the divorce in a healthy, honest and healing manner.

Kathy is an eleven year old girl who makes straight A's, is on the swim team, and has many friends. She is often invited to sleep-overs and is considered the most popular girl in her class.

Kathy's mother, Sue, told her in May that she was filing for a divorce from Kathy's father, Leo. Kathy had no real warning that things were that bad in her parents' marriage. By June, one month later, Sue and her three children had moved to another house ten blocks from their family home. Leo has been devastated by the sudden loss of his family. His pain is obvious, but he is trying to maintain frequent, friendly contact with the children.

When asked what had been most difficult thing for her during this split of the family, Kathy says "nothing." Prodded a little to see if she felt concerned or worried about her Dad or Mom, Kathy continues smiling and says "No, they are just fine." Kathy exhibits strong use of denial and repression. Right now the pain is so great, the events so confusing, the needs of her parents so conflicting, that she must use these techniques to continue in the progression and development of her own life. Kathy is protecting herself. Kathy's parents must go very slowly in introducing and discussing divorce-related issues with her, but they would be making a great mistake if they believe that she has no concerns or reactions related to the divorce.

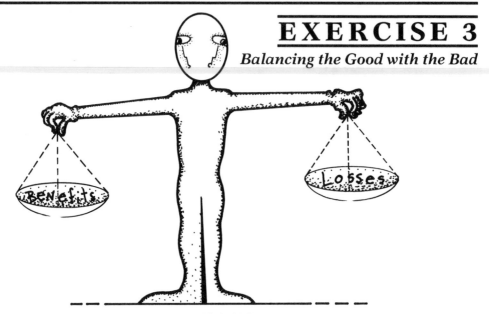

EXERCISE 3

Balancing the Good with the Bad

FOR YOU

Take a large piece of paper and across the top of it write: "My Divorce." Write the names of each family member, including your former spouse, across the page. Under each family member list losses and benefits of the divorce for that family member, as you see them.

(JULIE'S EXAMPLE)

MY DIVORCE

LOSSES

JULIE (32)	BOB (34)	TEDDY (9)	JOSH (6)
1. Income from Bob, when he worked.	1. Family to come come home to.	1. Living with daddy.	1. Living with daddy.
2. Sexual partner.	2. Some self-esteem.	2. Dad as base-ball coach.	2. A room alone.
3. Playmate for the boys.	3. Less contact with the boys.	3. Moved.	
4. Sold family home.	4. Julie to help out and to talk to.	4. Friends in old school.	
	5. Income—must pay child support.	5. Dad is unhappy.	
	6. Sexual partner.		

BENEFITS

1. Less worry about bills, I know what will come in.	1. Less pressure.	1. Fewer fights at home.	1. Fewer fights at home.
2. Don't have to nag.		2. Mom is happier.	2. New school.
3. Freedom to make decisions.			

(COMMENT)

Julie is a young divorced mother. It is clear that for this family Bob, her former husband, and Teddy, their nine year old son, are in the most pain. This helped Julie to understand why she felt so guilty when Teddy cried about his Dad no longer living with them. It also illustrated that the divorce did not affect both children in the family in the same way. Six year old Josh had few playmates in his old neighborhood. When they moved he found many friends in his new school. Julie did not lose her role of a full time homemaker (for some mothers this is a big loss), because she was already employed. Julie has listed more losses for Bob and fewer benefits for him than any family member. This might help her realize why she and her children feel sorry for Bob, although Julie must avoid the temptation to try to interfere in Bob's new life.

EXERCISE FOR AGES 6-8

Have a separate piece of paper for each family member, including your child's other parent, plus some magic markers. At the top of each sheet, print the name of every family member in a different color. Your child may want to print the names himself or herself. After the names are printed, ask your child to draw a picture of the biggest change each person has had to make since the divorce.

Your child may need some help thinking about the changes parents, brothers and sisters have had to make. Giving an example or two may stimulate his or her thinking. While your child is drawing, you may find it helpful and fun to draw your own pictures of changes that family members have made.

After your child has finished the drawings, look at each picture and ask the child to tell you what they mean. Are the changes primarily losses or gains? How does your child think each person might feel about the changes. For example, if the child drew a picture of Dad's new apartment, the child may say that Dad may feel lonely. If you have drawn your own pictures, you might share them with the child. Perhaps you discussion will end with you summarizing that it seems that all of the family members have undergone changes, but that in time everyone can get used to the way things are now.

EXERCISE FOR AGES 9-11

You will need a twelve inch ruler, a narrow-mouthed glass, and about 15 nickels or equivalent-weight chips. Balance the ruler across the top of the glass.

Explain to your child that he or she is going to try to balance what is "good" and "bad" about your divorce in his or her life. For each positive consequence of the divorce he or she can think of, one nickel or chip is balanced on one end of the ruler. For each negative thing, a nickel or chip is put on the other side.

Your child will have a lot of fun as one side or the other builds up and finally tips the ruler over—sending the nickels or chips flying! At this point, you can encourage your child to think of things on the opposite side of the scale which might balance the ruler off. This will allow you to help a child who sees the divorce too bleakly to recognize some positive changes in his or her life. For the child who is not acknowledging his or her hurt, this exercise will give permission to admit that there have been negative effects of the divorce in his or her life.

If the child enjoys the game, you can let him or her play again—using the effects of the divorce on other people in the family. As you help your child do this exercise, you will get new insights into how his or her perception of the consequences of the divorce differs from yours. If the child wants to discuss these changes, do so. . .perhaps sharing some of your thoughts. Be careful not to push your own feelings onto the child, however. His or her reactions or observations are not necessarily the same as yours. It is important that he or she be allowed to express these ideas freely.

CHAPTER 4

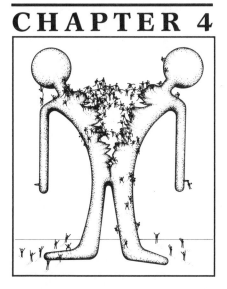

KNOWING YOUR CHILD

"Each child in my class is unique. . .each has strengths and weaknesses. I've been teaching third grade for fifteen years and every year has a personality. . .but you know, there are some things about third graders that are always the same."

Connie, a third grade teacher.

Unless you work professionally with children, you as a parent may not be familiar with the various stages of child development. Between the ages of ten and eleven, for example, many children will suddenly become more boisterous—much to their parents' chagrin! Yet this is a perfectly normal development in their growth and maturing process.

On the other hand, child work professionals—like teachers, social workers, youth ministers, sports coaches—often recognize before the parents themselves when a particular child is exhibiting behavior possibly indicating personal problems. These problems *may or may not* be related to a parental divorce.

Within any age group there are wide individual variations, yet there are some basic characteristics that are remarkably similar. For you to understand and help your school age child adjust to your divorce, it is important to spend sometime thinking about the characteristics of all school age children and then to identify the unique characteristics of each of your own children.

Ages six through eleven is a period of learning and growing—intellectually, spiritually, physically, and socially. Contact with the world outside the home (school, friends, and activities) becomes increasingly important and influential. Differences between boys and girls continue to emerge. Each child has a unique individual physical make-up and developmental history. This personal, social and genetic history will influence how a child responds to school, friends, and activities; it will also influence how a child responds to divorce.

SCHOOL

The years that a child spends in grade school mark a period of great skill growth. When you think of what a child entering first grade knows (or doesn't know) contrasted with what a sixth grader knows, one of the main developmental themes of this age period emerges—cognitive growth. Your child leaves home every day to spend six to seven hours in school. This is often more waking time than is spent at home. During the hours at school children learn to read and spell, begin to understand abstract math concepts, and discover new ways of looking at the world. To feel good about themselves, it is important for children to master the new material being presented in school. If your child cannot master much of the age-appropriate school material, then he or she may begin to develop self-doubts and experience anxiety.

Of course, every child cannot excel at everything. One child loves to read, another is good at math, a third may enjoy making maps and learning about birds' nests. The critical issue in development is that a child feels "good enough" about those things that he or she is mastering at school that the classroom environment feels comfortable.

In addition to academic learning, the school offers other critical experiences for the developing child: learning the social skills of interacting with peers and being able to accept the authority of adults other than the parent. Learning to function as an adult means knowing how to get along with others. This includes being able to work cooperatively with authority figures, the ability to give and take in group situations, and knowing how to maintain individual beliefs in the face of peer opposition. The interaction in school is the perfect laboratory for learning these social skills.

When parents divorce, one of the first places the stress of the divorce may show up for children is in the school setting. The child's school work will often slip, he or she may withdraw from friends or begin to get into fights on the playground, or there may be open defiance against the teacher. These are all clues that a child is experiencing changes or difficulties at home. This is true whether a child comes from a "divorced" or an "intact" family.

Over half of the school age children display some problems in school during the first year following a parental separation. After the first year, most children return to their pre-divorce level of school functioning. This means if your child was an average student with only a few friends before the divorce stress, that will be the level to which that particular child can be expected to return. In a few situations where the pre-divorce home environment was especially chaotic, the child's school behavior and performance may actually improve. For a small percentage of children, the decline in school may persist for a period longer than a year. Many of these children are caught in an ongoing parental conflict. For these children, the divorce has made matters worse.

During the time parents are experiencing tension, sadness and anger, school may actually be a welcome haven for some children. At school, things have remained the same. The teacher still makes you stay in from recess if you don't finish your math paper, spelling tests are still on Friday, and playing kick ball at recess is still fun. At school, no one usually knows what is happening at home . . . so certain children may become especially involved in learning and doing, thus having several hours of emotional peace from the turmoil at home. In this respect, a school age child is more fortunate than a younger child, who does not have as many challenging things to do and think about.

It is generally a good idea to tell the classroom teacher about your situation so that if school problems develop you can be notified. Many teachers report that they find it very helpful to know that a child's parents are in the process of a divorce so they can be sensitive and supportive in the classroom. If you decide to tell your child's teacher, be sure you let your child know so he or she won't feel that you and the teacher have secretly talked about private family matters. Many children are very sensitive about others knowing their parents are divorcing. By telling the teacher about the divorce and informing your child that you have done so, you are setting an example of how to deal openly and honestly with the divorce.

FRIENDS AND ACTIVITIES

In addition to school, friends and activities become increasingly important in a pre-adolescent child's life—whether their parents are divorced or not. The children of one divorced couple I worked with would be typical of any children this age: eight year old Jake was at soccer practice three afternoons a week, Cub Scouts one evening, and Sunday school; his nine year old sister Mary had choir practice, painting class, swimming lessons twice a week and Sunday school.

The expansion of skills—sports, crafts, outdoors—beyond the school setting is a natural development for grade school children. In these activities a child may have a chance to express creativity, cope with competition, and learn to follow complex rules.

Friends can be another important source of strength for your child during your divorce. Just as time at school may be a safe time, time with friends can be a fun time. If an eleven year old is thoroughly engaged in a swimming race, he or she will not necessarily be thinking about all of the disruptive changes at home.

If children are too sad or too anxious about problems at home, they may not have the energy to participate in the usual activities of others their age. This behavior is a sign that a particular child is in need of more support, communication and security.

Sometimes when parents divorce the budget cannot be stretched to include funds for children's extra activities. If you find yourself in the position of not having enough money for the usual swimming lessons or Girl Scouts, swallow your pride and talk to the leaders or teachers. Many organizations have special funds to help single parents in this type of crisis. If there isn't a "helping" fund perhaps you could ask a grandparent or special aunt or uncle to help pay for camp or dancing lessons.

Do not push your children into activities, but do try to keep their lives as much like it was before the divorce as possible. Remember there have been, and will continue to be, many changes and losses that you cannot prevent, so do try to keep their lives as "normal" as possible.

DIFFERENCES BETWEEN BOYS AND GIRLS

By the time your child enters school, you will begin to notice differences between the behavior of boys and that of girls. Boys are often better at abstract reasoning, they tend to play in groups and their play reveals they often fight over rules. The main emotion boys display is anger.

Grade school girls often show more openness verbally than boys of the same age. When girls have a problem they usually will want to talk about it. Girls may break down in tears when frustrated, angry or sad. School age girls usually have one or two "best" friends.

There are ongoing debates about whether the differences between boys and girls are basic inborn biological differences or if the differences are learned by being treated as a "boy" or a "girl." There is probably some truth in each school of thought. Every child is born with a basic biological make-up which will influence development, but as the child interacts with others he or she learns ways of behaving which insure acceptance.

Regardless of how each of your children has developed into being the person he or she is today, it is important to keep in mind that boys and girls may respond very differently to the divorce. Boys tend to deny or repress dealing with the divorce. They just don't want to talk about it and often wish for parental reconciliation. When boys do express their feelings toward the divorce, the emotion they use is many times the one they know best—anger: anger at their parents, other children, teachers, or the world in general. Boys may show their concern by getting in trouble in school or breaking and stealing things.

Girls, more often than boys, will want to understand and discuss the divorce. Girls may express a variety of feelings, such as relief and sadness. Symptoms of trouble with the divorce which grade school girls exhibit include: stomach aches, occasional loss of hair, bad dreams, problems with friends.

None of this means, of course, that your own children should or will respond in a stereotypical manner. There are many individual variations in the way boys and girls react to divorce. One ten year old boy, Sean, for example, is extremely verbal and expressive about his parents' divorce. Sean has expressed disappointment and sadness over his Dad leaving. He shared with many his feelings about having to move in with grandparents, and he has been worried and concerned about the well-being of both parents. Sean has wanted to talk long and often about the divorce with his parents, his counselor and others.

Marcy, a seven year old, on the other hand, shows intense anger about her parents' divorce by hitting her mother and destroying property. She keeps her thoughts about the divorce walled up inside. Marcy has refused to talk with either parent about her feelings and will not cooperate with a counselor.

PREVIOUS LOSSES

A loss or trauma always creates some stress. When someone suffers many losses and/or traumas, his or her body, mind and spirit may have difficulty managing the accumulated stress. For young children, this effect is more pronounced because they have so few experiences to give them perspective.

By the time you decided to divorce, your pre-adolescent child had only a few years of life. Some of his or her experiences may help your child adjust to your divorce, while others may have created a vulnerability that will result in him or her having a more difficult time adjusting to the divorce.

It is important, therefore, to consider what losses—prior to the divorce—each individual child has experienced. How has the family responded to these losses? How has the child responded? Two common losses that many children may have experienced at this age are death of a grandparent, an aunt or uncle, the parent of a friend; and moving—which results in the loss of friends, loss of school and loss of familiar surroundings. Other losses which are less common—but very traumatic—are death of a friend or classmate, health problems, previous parental divorce, destruction of the family home by fire or flood, and loss of family status and security when the family breadwinner is unemployed for a long period.

Of the common losses most children experience, the death of a pet almost always results in intense, sad feelings. Even some college students describe the death of their dog or cat as the most traumatic event of their childhood. (If you are thinking about giving the family pet away after your divorce to save money or to comply with an apartment lease, remember that it will create an additional loss for your child. If there is no way you can keep the pet, make every attempt to find a new home, so that your child is assured of its well-being.)

One remarkable and complicating characteristic of human beings is that they respond so differently to similar events. One child may be thrilled with moving to a new home because there were no friends the same age in the previous neighborhood. Another child may long for years for the "old neighborhood." If a child has been very close to a grandparent, the death of this person will result in sadness and mourning. If the grandparent was hardly known to the child, however, the grandparent's death would not result in a feeling of loss but would simply become an objective fact the child knows: "My grandfather is dead."

Children are very sensitive to their parents' responses to changes. If the death of your parent has been very upsetting for you, for example, your child will likely also have intense feelings about the experience. This is not to suggest that you should mask your feelings, but become aware that your feelings influence your child. When my daughter was two years old a very close friend of mine, Sandy, moved to Atlanta. Sandy and I had been supportive friends for several years, and her move felt like the loss of a family member. When I suffer a loss, I usually react by becoming quiet and withdrawn—trying internally to understand what has happened and to comfort myself. I usually do not cry or openly express grief. When Sandy told me she was moving I felt shocked and sick, but outwardly I just appeared quiet and strained. My daughter, Karla, picked up on my sadness and decided I needed to be cheered up. For days she would dance around the living room, doing somersaults, performing. She knew something important had happened to me, and she wanted to help me.

Previous losses will influence your child's responses to the current changes your divorce creates. If your child has had *no* previous losses, the divorce may seem devastating. If your child has had previous losses that remain unresolved, the pain of the divorce may be magnified. If your child has shown resiliency and adaptability in responding to previous losses, then he or she may draw upon these same strengths in adjusting to the divorce.

PHYSICAL INFLUENCES

Emotional stress created by the divorce places demands upon the body, which may result in the child developing symptoms of a whole range of physical problems. Children who are fortunate enough to be healthy can count on their own

44

natural physical energy to help them in times of stress. Children who have health problems prior to their parents' divorce, however, are more likely to become ill than the healthy child. Children who cope daily with physical problems such as allergies, learning disabilities, hyperactivity, hearing or vision loss, or diabetes may experience more difficulty during parental divorce. So much of their natural energies are already being used up in compensating for their physical condition.

Dawn was ten when her parents, Zeik and Alana, divorced. Dawn had suffered from allergies since she was two. When her parents were in the process of divorce, these allergies became much worse. During one month, Alana had to rush Dawn to the hospital twice with asthma attacks. Dawn was crabby with her friends and always seemed very tired. Zeik and Alana spent hours in the doctor's office with her. Dawn's eight year old sister Toni, who was experiencing the same stress and losses as Dawn, coped much better. Toni was an energetic, healthy girl, and although she felt upset when her parents fought and was sad when they had to sell the house, she did not become ill.

THE PAYOFF

The ability to get to know each of your children intimately as a real, unique human being is the most important asset that you can have as a parent in helping them through your divorce. A growing closeness between you and each child may be one of the few immediate and tangible benefits of the divorce. Make the most of it.

* * *

EXERCISE 4

Doing the Puzzle That Is Your Child

FOR YOU

You will need a large piece of paper. Across the top of the paper write "My Children." Under this heading draw a symbolic representation of each child. For example, if your daughter is generally sweet and cooperative you might draw a flower; on the other hand, if she is lanky and active you might draw a young colt. Don't worry about your artistic capabilities, just have fun thinking of a symbol for each child. Under each symbol print each child's full name.

Under the name of each child, list his or her specific abilities, interests, and limits. Next list three specific things you can do to encourage a strength or help with a weakness. After you have completed this exercise, think about which of your plans for your child you can carry out in the next two weeks.

(MARY KAY'S EXAMPLE)

MY CHILDREN

	(tornado)	(teddy bear)
	MARIE ANN (10)	JANA KAY (7)
ABILITIES	• Very good student, especially in reading • Good eye for color • Excellent runner	• Makes friends easily • Laughs • Cooperates at school

(continued)

INTERESTS	• Girl Scouts • Animals • Board games • Being outside	• TV quiz shows • Cooking • Animals • Brownies
LIMITS	• Messy • Volatile, angers easily • Sometimes impatient with teachers, sister and friends	• Learning disability, affects reading • A little overweight

WHAT CAN I DO TO HELP?

FOR MARIE:

1. Sign her up for art lessons at the Park District.

2. Try to be patient with her, so she can learn patience.

3. Spend a half hour a week helping her organize her room. Let her do most of it, but make it a fun time for both of us.

FOR JANA:

1. Get her a children's cook book and together cook a nutritional low calorie meal once a week.

2. Encourage her to get involved in more physical activities: for example, enroll her in swimming lessons.

3. Spend twenty minutes an evening reading with her.

(COMMENT)

When Mary Kay, the girls' mother, did this exercise, she had some difficulty coming up with three things she could do to help Marie. Yet it was easy for her to plan things with Jana.

Mary Kay wanted Marie to learn to control her temper, but wanted to avoid nagging her or punishing her. Finally she decided to try to model patience for her.

Jana has an outgoing, easy personality, but Mary Kay was concerned about her tendency to be overweight. Mary Kay decided to help both herself and Jana learn more about nutrition by planning good, low calorie meals together. She also thought they would have fun working together in the kitchen.

Notice that all the plans will require time and effort on Mary Kay's part. When parents are in the process of divorce they often feel overwhelmed. Adding anything to the many things that already need to be done may seem unreasonable. Yet children need special consideration and attention at this time.

EXERCISE FOR AGES 6-8

Take out three pieces of construction paper, white or different colors. You will also need paste, scissors and several old magazines or catalogs. On the top of each sheet of paper, print one of the categories: "Good At," "I Like," and "Help!" Then ask your child to look through the magazines and cut out pictures of things her or she can do well, things he or she is interested in, and things he or she has difficulty with.

At first, the child may not think there are many things he or she does well, but you can help by pointing out how good he is at feeding the cat or she is at riding her bicycle. Help your child understand each category and if needed give a suggestion or two, but do not take the "thinking and doing" away.

After the pages are completed, have your child star the ability, interest and limit that he or she feels is most important. Place the completed papers on the refrigerator or in the special folder.

EXERCISE FOR AGES 9-11

You will need a large sheet of butcher paper (the size of your child) and magic markers, or some colored chalk.

Have your child lie on the piece of paper or on the basement floor. You outline his or her entire body with the marker or chalk. Now have your child get up and fill in the outline. Using one color marker or chalk, have the child list inside the outlined head all the things he or she is good at. In a second color, have him or her list inside the body (around the heart) those things that he or she likes or is interested in. Finally, ask the child to list outside the body in a third color all those things he or she has difficulty with.

This exercise will help your children look at themselves and will also give you insights into each child. If a child is having trouble getting started, you might have him or her outline your body first and help you do the exercise on yourself. Your vulnerability and willingness to share will encourage your child to do the same.

If there is no room or materials to outline entire bodies, you can substitute the outline of a hand, with abilities listed in the fingers, interests in the palm and limits outside the hand itself.

CHAPTER 5

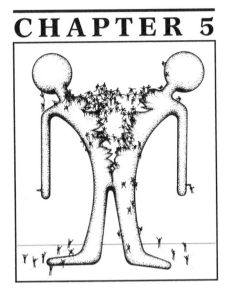

DIFFERENT FAMILIES

" I'm embarrassed to tell my friends that my parents are getting a divorce, so I'm just not asking anyone over to our house. Then they will never know."

Nora, an eleven year old girl.

In the years preceding the divorce, your family developed a unique and interesting history. It began when you and your former spouse met and were courting. It continued to build, marked by important events such as your wedding, setting up a household, the birth of children, and perhaps the purchase of a home and a move to a different community.

Over time you developed important family rituals and ways to celebrate. Birthdays, Christmas or Hanukkah, Thanksgiving and Easter are holidays that your family probably celebrated in special ways. These are memories you all—including your children's other parent—share. You may remember such events with fondness, and it may make you feel sad or angry that they will not be able to be celebrated by the same people in the same way ever again. Your children will have their own feelings—which may or may not mirror your own.

There are also everyday rituals that your pre-divorce family shared that may now have to change. Perhaps your family always went out for pizza on Friday night, roasted corn on hot summer days, gave tiny children shiny quarters when they lost a tooth, and went grocery shopping every Thursday night. Although these events may not seem as important as special holidays, they give a family its own identity.

Family identity is more than individual family rituals and routines, however. It includes the certainty that each member is attached to the same family roots. These roots include an attachment to family names, family history and folklore, and perhaps even a family hometown. People, and especially young people, want to feel proud of their family roots.

When a divorce takes place, there is often a ripping apart of attachments made to the "other half" of the family identity or roots. Both parents and children are suddenly cut off from seeing people who prior to the divorce had played important roles in their lives. Some children even lose the name-connection to their mother if she resumes her maiden name after the divorce. Understanding that you and your children have suffered a major blow to family and personal identity is a major step in beginning to rebuild and solidify a sense of pride and identity in the post-divorce family.

Your children may also be affected by how those close to them and others in the community react to the divorce. Thus, the process of rebuilding a strong sense of family identity should include an awareness of how divorce, divorced people and children from divorced families are perceived by "important others."

CHANGING ROUTINES

As special events and holidays arise, you and your children must decide if you will continue doing things as you have in the past or will change your family rituals. Maybe you went shopping on Thursday nights because that was the day your former spouse was paid, but now you receive your child support check at the first of the month and are paid on the 15th and 30th of the month. It may be easier to shop on Friday nights or Sunday afternoons, so you change that routine.

The family may have gone out for pizza on Friday because everyone was tired from the week and wanted to celebrate in a small way the start of the weekend. You might still want to celebrate making it through the week, but you might no longer have your children with you every weekend. Perhaps you could make another evening during the week a "special night" for you and your children. When your children are away, make plans to do something different for yourself. Go to a shopping center and take time to look through a new bookstore, go bowling, visit a friend, or buy yourself one of the new frozen dinners and watch T.V. in bed. Try to recognize when a change of family routines is going to be painful and plan and build new, helpful routines for yourself and your children.

In the first years following the separation, each special event or season will bring up memories of what the family was doing at that time the previous year.

Some of these memories may be bittersweet because at the time the event was pleasant and now things have changed so dramatically. In the spring you recall how cute your six year old son looked out in the back yard learning to throw a baseball with his Dad, your former husband. Or your daughter gives you a look while you are bowling that reminds you of the way your former wife used to look at you when you were on a team together. These same experiences are happening all the time to your children.

Other memories may not be very pleasant. You recall how you had to fill the children's Christmas stockings alone because your wife (or husband) had drunk six glasses of wine and had passed out on the couch; or you remember taking the children to church alone on Easter because your husband (or wife), "Just had to play golf." Children also have memories that make them feel sad and lonely. Both you and your children need time to mourn the loss of the pre-divorce family. It is very important for you to allow your child the opportunity to do this mourning. Your child may say,"Dad (or Mom), remember how funny it was when Mom (or Dad) spilled the spaghetti sauce on Grandma?" This is an indication that your child is reviewing, in his or her mind some aspect of your family life before the divorce. If you react to these comments in a negative way, such as "That was a long time ago and I don't want to talk about it," or "Yes, your Mom (or Dad) certainly is clumsy." Then you are communicating that conversation about the pre-divorce family is unwelcome.

We mourn by remembering and reminiscing. In the first year or two after the separation, expect your child to want to talk about things as they "used to be." Over time this type of reminiscing will diminish. You and your children will have developed a new family style that includes aspects of the pre-divorce family but also includes new rituals and routines. Your former spouse should have done the same.

SOCIETAL CHANGES

At the same time your children are in the process of mourning the loss of the pre-divorce family, they will be influenced and affected by how others view divorce and divorced families. I am in my mid-forties, and when I was growing up in a small town in Illinois and later in a suburb of Chicago, not one of my friends was living in single parent homes, none were living in remarried families and very few mothers worked outside the home. Today, many marriages end in divorce, a large percentage of children spend some time living in a single parent home, and most women have jobs outside the home. Being divorced or living in a single parent home is no longer atypical. Parental divorce is an event that many children will experience. If they do not personally experience the divorce of their parents, they will often be close to a divorced family.

51

As an event becomes more and more common, the stigma attached to it often becomes less prominent. It would seem likely that since divorce is becoming a more common occurrence, children and their parents would feel little stigma or shame if the parents do divorce. This is often not the case, however. Many children are very ashamed of what has happened to their families and feel as if they are the only ones in the world (or at least in their classroom) that come from a "broken home."

Why is there this discrepancy between the social reality—many divorces—and the personal reality—a child feeling that they are so different from others? How children view divorce and living in a single parent home depends on several variables: where the family lives, what types of families they have known, how their parents viewed divorced families as they were growing up, and how their parents now view themselves and their family.

GEOGRAPHIC LOCATION

Some parts of the country have much higher divorce rates than others. Urban areas, especially areas that are experiencing high rates of growth, have exceptionally high divorce rates. In the early 1970's, California was the trend setter for divorce. . .some children living in urban California cities such as San Francisco or Los Angles complained that their families were "different" if the parents were not divorced. It was not that these children actually wanted their parents to divorce, but in their schools and among their friends it was more the norm to be from a divorced home than an intact family.

In the early 1980's, New Mexico and Oklahoma were two states with very high divorce rates (only Nevada and Alaska had higher divorce rates). Some social scientists believe the high divorce rates in these states were a result of people migrating to boom areas where there was rapid economic growth in the energy industry. Texas has replaced California with "eye opening" statistics: there was an almost 60% increase in the divorce rate in Texas from the early 1960's to the 1980's. It appears that relocation and the loss of traditional family roots creates stress for families, and this stress often results in parental divorce.

Other parts of the country—especially rural areas and small towns—have lower than average divorce rates. These more traditional areas may be located within a state that has an overall high divorce rate. Within any one state or geographic region there will be wide variations of family experiences.

If you live in an area with a high divorce rate, the chances are more likely that your child will know other children from divorced families. The classroom teacher or soccer coach might even be divorced. Thus, even though your divorce will still be difficult for your child, he or she may gain some comfort from seeing that others who are respected and liked in the community are also affected by divorce. If you live in an area where there are very few divorces, your child may indeed be the only one from a divorced home in the classroom. This will increase the likelihood of your child feeling different. To get a better idea of what your child is experiencing at school and in the community, spend a little time investigating the facts. Talk to the school principal. Ask how many children in your child's classroom are living in single parent homes or remarried families. Of course, the principal will not give you the names of those families, for that information is confidential. He or she can, however, provide you with general numbers. Talk to the leader of the scout troop or coach of the baseball team and ask if any of the children are from divorced families.

After you have this information you can share it with your child. If there are several children from divorced families at school and in activities you may say, "I talked to Mr. Strehlow, the principal of your school, and he said that in your room there are four other children who live with just their mother, one who lives with her father, and two children whose parents have been divorced but are now remarried. Mr. Stanley, the baseball coach, said both Ralph and Jimmy are from divorced families. I know it doesn't make you feel any better about Mom and I getting divorced, but at least you know that our family is not so unusual."

If you find out there are very few children from divorced families you might say, "I talked with Mrs. Bloomquist, the school nurse, and she said only one other child in fourth grade is from a divorced family, and that child has the other fourth grade teacher. I know our family now is different from other families because Dad doesn't live here any more, but we still are a nice family. Dad and I both care for you, and we both will do things with you."

Both of these statements are telling your child that you are sensitive to the fact that being from a divorced family may result in some uncomfortable feelings. This kind of communication is empathetic and brief, but it has a clear message. This is an excellent way to introduce other divorce related topics. Notice that the child was not forced to say anything and that blame was not place on anyone, but the message did not "gloss over" the reality.

OTHER FAMILIES

People tend to gravitate toward people who are similar to them. Married couples with children usually socialize with other married couples with children. These friendships may begin when the parents meet in child related activities such as church, school P.T.A., or scouts. Single parents are often employed and have many additional responsibilities to keep the family running. They may have less time to be involved in outside activities. If a single parent does have free time, he or she may want to engage in activities with other single adults.

Most children who are from nuclear families do not spend much time with divorced, single parent families. Even though there might be divorces in their extended family, children still think of a "family" as a mother, father and children—all living together. When divorce causes your family to become different from the "normal" family, your child may begin to feel stigmatized. This feeling may be reinforced by other children.

Adrianne is an attractive, cheerful and quick fifth grader, qualities that usually result in many friendships. "Most of the girls in my class don't like me," she claims. "They say I'm poor now, and that since we have to live with my grandma no one wants to come to my house anymore." Adrianne's parents divorced a year ago, and the family has lost their home and financial reserves in the process. In some respects Adrianne's family *was* poor, at least at this time. But, Adrianne and her two brothers were not poor in emotional support. Her parents, Jill and Dave, although divorced, worked cooperatively with the children. Their children felt loved and cared for. They dressed like all the other children in the school, for the school they attended required the children to wear uniforms. Where had Adrianne's classmate come up with such a cruel judgment? They had overheard adults talking about the divorce. In Adrianne's small school, being from a divorced family still seemed to be unusual.

It is important for you to explore with your child the many variations of families which exist, illustrating that many families are not like the "average American family" portrayed in textbooks and in the media. Variations include two married people without children . . . they are a family; an elderly person living with an adult child . . . they are a family; parents with foster children . . . they are a family; two persons formerly married who have remarried . . . they are a family. Your children will probably be upset over the loss of the pre-divorce family for a long time, but helping them accept many styles of families will be a step in accepting their new family.

PARENTS' ATTITUDES TOWARD DIVORCE

You need to show your children by your own words and actions that your new family is a real family! Reflecting on your own attitudes and feelings may help you understand what your child is going through.

Before you were divorced, you and your former spouse had attitudes toward divorce and toward children from divorced homes. These attitudes were expressed in subtle ways that now may be influencing how your child feels about being from a divorced family. If you felt divorce was an unfortunate event that was sad for all family members—but that the divorce did not automatically make people immoral, troubled or bad—then your children probably exhibit similar attitudes. On the other hand, if either or both of you felt uneasy about your child playing with a child from a single parent family or remarked, "Oh isn't he (or she) the one whose parents are divorced," when you heard of a teenager who got picked up for drunk driving, then your children probably have very negative feelings toward divorced families.

Mark was very agitated and angry when he found out that his parents, Melissa and Martin, were going to be divorced. He dissolved into tears, "Now I'm going to be like all of those other children from divorced families." "How are they?" he was asked. "Oh you know, they get poor grades and always drop out of school."

Melissa had a predominantly neutral attitude toward divorce, but Martin felt very much the way Mark did. The father believed that divorce would instantly turn anyone's child into a neurotic misfit. His attitude was transmitted almost completely to his son.

Parental divorce can be so stressful that a child may experience some, or even many, adjustment problems following parental separation. These adjustment problems are not necessarily long lasting or forever debilitating. *A divorce does not have to overshadow the long standing strengths and resources the family has possessed.*

If a child graduates with honors, is elected class president, or becomes a star basketball player, you never hear people say, "This great accomplishment is because the parents are divorced." Yet if a child gets into trouble with the law, abuses drugs, or becomes pregnant before marriage, such behavior is often blamed on the parental divorce. If you have transmitted negative feelings about divorce to your child, perhaps you could begin to neutralize some of these negative messages. Remember that it is important for children to feel good about their families, whether divorced or intact.

You might say something like this, "Before Mom (or Dad) and I were divorced I used to think that divorce was so awful that it would ruin everyone in the family. Now that we are a divorced family I see that I was wrong. Divorce is certainly painful and confusing, but I still think we are good people and still have a nice family. I guess I really didn't know enough about divorce before this happened to us." This is a short clear message, not filled with blame or shame. It can help your children feel more hopeful about their family and the future. Only say something like this to your child if you mean it, however, for if the words are hollow your children will sense it and feel even more uneasy and worried about the divorce.

The location of your home, community attitudes, the types of families you know, as well as your former spouse's attitude and your own attitude toward divorce in general will affect how your child views divorce. Perhaps the factor that has the strongest effect on your child's attitude, however, is how you are feeling about what happened to your family and to you personally. Divorce often comes as a shock, and you may be left feeling disillusioned and frightened. Some parents become so angry and upset that these feelings take over their whole being.

There are women who complain, for example, "Why did he do this to me! I do not want to go out to work. I got married to stay home and raise children. That is the life we agreed to." There are men who say, "How could she break the marriage promise? It was a commitment. It is unfair that I am losing my home and my children and I have no choice in the matter. My choice was to stay married!"

These are normal and understandable responses to an event—divorce—that was not anticipated and often not wanted by one of the parties. If you become stuck in one of these pessimistic, victimized, angry stances for too long, however, it will have a negative effect on you and most especially on your children. If you dwell on the injustice of your divorce, people will begin to drift away from you. Even your children may pull back. As they and others stay away, you will feel even more angry and more victimized: "No one really cares that my life has been ruined." This vicious cycle will continue until you break it. If you cannot do it for yourself, do it for your children.

If you want to move forward but feel that you are having difficulty doing it, you may want to get outside help. Local churches and mental health centers often sponsor divorce adjustment or support groups. Participating in these discussion groups might help you resolve some of your pain and fear. If you are hesitant to join a divorce group, arrange to talk to the leader. He or she can explain what the group is like and assure you that you only need to talk when and if you feel comfortable. Even if you cannot share very much about your own divorce, you can gain a lot by listening to others' stories.

If there is no divorce group in your area call a priest, minister, rabbi, or your local mental health center and ask what types of services are available for divorcing families. Reaching out for help will be a big step in helping you in the process of healing and rebuilding, and it is the best single thing that you can do to help your children adapt to the divorce.

* * *

EXERCISE 5

Painting Your New Family Portrait

FOR YOU

Across the top of a large piece of paper write "My Family Before the Divorce" and divide the paper into three columns. In column one write "Activities I Will Miss." Under this heading list the special celebrations and rituals you will miss. Title the next column "Feelings" and cite how it makes you feel to lose this special family routine. Column three is to be headed "Possible Solutions" and here you should list your alternatives to the lost activity.

(EVA'S EXAMPLE)
MY FAMILY BEFORE THE DIVORCE

I WILL MISS	FEELINGS	POSSIBLE SOLUTIONS
1. Gil taking the children to chop Christmas tree.	Anger at Gil, sad feelings for the children.	a. Take the children myself. b. Purchase a tree for our house. c. Ask Gil if he will still take the children, but take the tree to his house.
2. In July going to the cabin we always rented.	Uncertain about my being able to go away with the children alone, afraid. Sad, that I won't see the cabin again.	a. Rent a similar cabin at a nearby lake. b. Do something; plan a trip to state capitol. c. Stay at home, but make a special effort to do some "vacation" type activities.

(continued)

57

3. Gil and the children bringing me breakfast in bed on Mother's Day.	Sad—resentful that we are not like other families.	a. Encourage the children to make me breakfast; get any special ingredients they need.
		b. Get up and go out for breakfast.
4. The family watching T.V. together on Saturday night.	Lonely, being with the children alone.	a. Allow myself to feel lonely.
		b. Go out to an early movie with the children.
		c. Make popcorn and watch T.V. with the children anyway, even if I am lonely.
		d. Call my mother or a friend.

(COMMENT)

Eva is a newly divorced woman with three children. Two events that Eva felt she would miss were associated with special holidays: Christmas and Mother's Day. One event was a seasonal happening, the family vacation, and one was the ongoing family routine of watching T.V. together. Eva discovered that she was still feeling angry at her former husband Gil for wanting the divorce, which created the need to change things in the family. As Eva wrote down her possible solutions, she found that there were things she could do to create new family routines. She also realized that her own feelings toward the divorce and toward Gil had stopped her from trying any solutions. After doing this exercise Eva was willing to try some of her ideas.

EXERCISE FOR AGES 6-8

Set out some poster paints. Be certain to have plenty of water and paper towels. (If you don't have paints your child can use markers. However, children love to paint, and just being able to paint may encourage your child to do the exercise.)

Ask your child to paint a picture of his or her family. The title of the picture should be "My Family." This exercise can be done with several children working together but be sure each child is allowed the freedom to paint the family as he or she wants. There is no right or wrong. Your child may ask if the other parent should be included. You should respond with, "You can put whoever you want in the picture."

Some children will include certain siblings, others will arrange the family by sex or age, some will paint the pre-divorce family, others will include grandparents and other extended family members, while still others will paint the new single parent family. However your child paints "My Family," this is how he or she perceives the family at this point in time.

As you look at the painting, be careful not to make your child feel defensive about who is, or who is not, included. For example, do not say, "Why didn't you include Dad?" or "Where is your Mom?" Get a feeling for what struggles the child may be having with the concept of the family. After the painting is complete you might display it on the refrigerator door or on the family room wall, or your child may wish to place it in the project folder. The picture could promote a discussion between you and your child about the changes in the family and what the child misses most about the family as it was before the divorce.

If you and your former spouse have a cooperative co-parenting relationship you might ask him or her to have the child draw or paint a family picture when visiting with that parent. It is best if at least two weeks have elapsed since the first painting. Having the child repeat the picture allows the child to express his or her sense of family in both family settings.

(A word of caution is in order. Only suggest the dual painting project if you and your former spouse have resolved major conflicts related to the children, otherwise one of you may be tempted to interpret the paintings in a way that will reinforce some current conflictive situation. Your child must *never* feel that you are using these exercises to gain information for a custody battle. These exercises are *only* to be done to help your children express themselves and to have fun.)

EXERCISE FOR AGES 9-11

You will need a large poster board, paste and some old family photos.

People of all ages want to know their family roots. Creating a simple family tree will help your child realize that although his or her parents are divorced, there will always be a real, physical connection to both.

To help your child create a simple family tree, have him or her draw a tree with roots and branches. Take the old photographs and paste pictures of both sets of grandparents in the roots of the tree. In the lower branches paste a picture of you and your former spouse, then in the upper branches have the child paste a picture of himself and pictures of all brothers and sisters. If there are older siblings who have married, include pictures of their spouses and children on the upper branches.

As you and your child work, not only talk about how divorce has changed your family but also about how your child will always be attached to his or her roots. You might want to suggest that the divorce has caused a split in the family tree between you and your former spouse, but that your children still *belong* to both sides of the family tree.

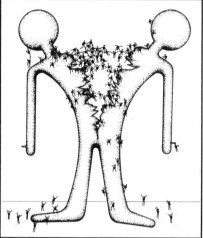

CHAPTER 6

CHILDREN'S RESPONSES TO DIVORCE

"Matt's teacher called and said she just doesn't know what to do with him. He is constantly causing problems in the classroom, talking to other children, acting silly and getting into fights. Besides disrupting the class he isn't getting any of his work done."

Jack, a divorced father.

Matt and Jenny, ages ten and six, were in their father's custody since their mother left ten months ago. The entire family had been shocked when the mother had announced that she was leaving the family and moving to another city to further her career and pursue a relationship with a work colleague. At first the father, Jack, was hardly aware of his children's feelings. He had so many new tasks and responsibilities thrust upon him. In addition to his own career, now Jack had to do all of those things his wife had done. . .wash the clothes, clean the house, take the children shopping for clothes and plan the meals.

Suddenly, Matt and Jenny began to experience symptoms related to the shock and loss they had experienced. Jenny had ongoing pains in her shoulders and neck and was waking up occasionally with nightmares. Matt's teacher called to complain to Jack about Matt's school behavior.

The reactions of Jack's children are typical of many children of divorced parents. Such reactions may emerge immediately after the parents separate or can develop a few months later. Parents and teachers may not even notice subtle changes for some time. Even after misbehavior begins, however, teachers will usually wait a week or two before calling a parent. They will continue to observe the child to see if this is just a "bad" week or if the change in behavior is something to be seriously concerned about. Parents will often dismiss health problems as normal "growing pains." In fact, all children have aches, pains, nightmares and problems in school. A parent may legitimately wonder whether problems are related to the divorce, to other events in the child's life, or are just a "phase." There is no easy answer to this dilemma, but the divorce as a potential cause of changes in a child's behavior or health must be taken into consideration.

Children's problems are often compounded by the differing perceptions of their two parents. The parent who initiated a divorce—who wanted or feels responsible for the divorce—has a tendency to overlook many of the problems children are experiencing or to suggest that these are normal, typical childhood problems. The parent who did not want the divorce or does not feel responsible for it often sees every problem the child has as related to the divorce. The truth usually lies in the middle of these two positions. Children are always affected by their parents' divorce. Most children will show some reactive behavior during the first year after the divorce and will continue to struggle with it for many years after. Yet not every problem—or every success, for that matter—a child has can be attributed to the divorce.

ANGER

A logical emotion for children to feel at the time of a major loss like divorce is anger. Whenever things are taken from us, or changed without our consent, there is a feeling of losing control of our own destiny. This makes us angry. Some children may express this anger very directly, "I hate Dad (or Mom) for leaving me!" Usually, however, children will express their anger in subtle, unclear ways; or they will target their anger at a person or object they feel can absorb it.

Peter was eleven when his parents separated. His mother noticed that Peter was becoming somewhat abusive to the family dog. He would hold the dog, Rex, very tight, and seemed happy when Rex became frustrated and upset. This sounds like such cruel behavior, yet Peter was basically a sensitive, kind boy. Why would he get pleasure in hurting a dog he really loved? The answer is that Peter was angry, especially at his mother whom he blamed for the divorce. He also loved his mother and needed her to take care of him. He did not feel safe and free to direct his anger at his mother. The dog became a "safe" target for his anger. Peter does to the dog what he feels has been done to him, but he is now the one in control of the hurting.

62

It is crucial to remember that children usually are not aware of *why* they are performing angry acts. Peter is not consciously hurting the dog because he cannot hurt his mother. In fact, when Peter's mother asked him, "Why are you teasing and hurting Rex?" Peter answered honestly, "I don't know." All Peter knows is that he feels sort of relieved after squeezing Rex. Peter certainly does not link the divorce to the dog. If such a connection were pointed out to him, Peter would probably think that this was the strangest thing he had ever heard: why would the divorce and his dog have anything to do with each other?

Matt, whose family situation was briefly described at the start of this chapter, was also feeling angry about his parents' divorce. He became overly talkative and aggressive at school, and he stopped doing his school work. Matt, like Peter, was showing that he had some control over things in his life. He could hit other boys and force them to notice him. He could rebel against the teacher and make her angry. He could not, however, be angry at his mother because then she might never come back—and Matt was secretly hoping that she would. Nor could he be angry at his father, because Dad was taking care of him. School became a safe target for his anger.

Sometimes a child will be angry at the custodial parent. This anger may be observed in such actions as not minding, talking back and arguing, calling the parent names, and even hitting the parent. This happens when the child misses the absent parent very much and blames the custodial parent for the loss. This blame, of course, is not justified, yet the child experiences the feeling just the same. One eleven year old girl, Becky, was extremely hostile to her mother, Teresa, blaming her for the father's absence. The father, Paul, was an abusive, alcoholic man who had caused his wife years of agony before she decided he would not change and filed for divorce. Becky yells at Teresa, "If only you had been nicer to Dad he would not have had to drink. You caused the divorce, and I hate your for it!" Becky cannot accept that Paul, by his actions, contributed to the deterioration of the family. She misses him too much, yet she is secure enough with her mother to vent anger on her; she really knows her mother will not leave her, and that her mother loves her. Becky is much less sure of her father's feelings or actions, and thus mother becomes the target for her anger.

FEAR

When the family begins to change, children become afraid. They quite literally fear for their own safety and survival. The fear that the child feels may not be rational, but it is real and based on feelings generated by the many changes. If one parent could leave, for example, it is now possible in the child's mind that the other parent could also leave, or even die. Then what would happen to the child?

In some instances, the fear the child feels may be based on reality: his or her well-being really is at risk. For example, if one parent has a tendency toward violent behavior, the child may fear that parent will hurt him or her or hurt other family members. If you have a history of violence yourself, please seek help immediately. Talk to a rabbi, minister or priest, or to a professional helper such as a social worker, psychologist or psychiatrist. These are people who are educated and trained to deal with people who lose control. If you feel that your former spouse could become violent with your child, consult your attorney.

Children may also feel fear when they observe one of their parents emotionally deteriorating. If the break-up of the family has triggered excessive drinking, severe depression, or extreme anxiety, a child may correctly perceive that the parent is not functioning as a mature adult and is unable to provide adequate care. If you have some questions about whether the divorce has affected you or your former spouse to this degree, discuss your concerns with a professional.

When parental separation triggers fear (even if not related to actual threats) in children, they will often express their fear in ways which do not seem at all divorce related. You, as a parent, will need to be the emotional interpreter of your child's concerns. Is this fear related to a real loss? If the answer is yes, then most likely the fear has been stimulated by the change in the family. Andy got a new puppy two months before his father, Walter, moved out of the family home. Every day when Andy's mother, Maria, picked him up from school he would ask her if the dog was dead. Andy was clearly expressing a fear about something else . . . something over which he had no control. Perhaps Andy was afraid that Maria, whom he now depended upon for survival, might die. This was an irrational fear, for both Andy's pet and his mother were very healthy. Even if something did happen to Andy's mother, Walter was a concerned, caring father who could take care of Andy very well. Yet inside this seven year old there was a fear of abandonment.

Children often feel comforted by the presence of a male in the house. Men have deep voices, are tall, and seem powerful to children. They derive a sense of security from a father whom they perceive as being strong, big, and safe. After the separation, some children who have never been afraid of robbers and murderers develop these fears and are afraid to go to sleep or to be alone. This is true even though the family may live in a very safe neighborhood and Mom may not be at all afraid.

SADNESS

Almost everyone in the family feels sad about a divorce. Even when there is a sense of general relief because a conflictive relationship has finally ended, there is usually also a sad feeling associated with the lost hopes and dreams of having a complete, happy family. When a child shows some sadness about the divorce, this feeling is usually understandable and acceptable to the parents.

The child may mope around the house, cry easily, not eat as usual, and seem to get little pleasure out of doing things that were formerly enjoyable. These are signs of depression, a kind of sadness and anger kept inside. Some children experience intense sadness and longing for the absent parent. This response may baffle the custodial parent who says, "I don't understand their crying for their father (or mother). When we were married my husband (or wife) was a workaholic and never home. The children have never been close to him (or her). What's going on?" The actual amount of contact with the non-custodial parent prior to the separation often has little to do with how much a child misses that parent. In fact, some children who have not spent much time with the absent parent are especially devastated by the departure because they now feel they will never get to know that parent.

Some children feel sad when they come home from visiting the non-custodial parent. Sadness is a natural response to leaving someone you care for. This is *not* a reason for the child to stop seeing the non-custodial parent. It merely means that at the end of a visitation, the custodial parent can anticipate sadness and be prepared to allow the child some transition time to readjust.

ANXIETY

Anxiety is an emotional response that sometimes results in the development of physical symptoms. Anxiety is a feeling of general uncertainty or uneasiness about what is going to happen. Many of the changes caused by divorce are beyond the control of a child. It makes sense that during, or following, parental divorce a child may exhibit signs of anxiety. Physical symptoms that may point to an underlying anxiety are headaches, bad dreams, stomach aches, loss of hair, biting nails, chewing lips, asthma attacks, bed wetting or dizziness.

If your child has recently developed any of these symptoms, the first step is to consult with your family physician. After the child has been given a clean bill of health, only your understanding and support can help reduce the anxious state.

Sometimes the child displays anxiety by being generally fidgety and restless. If your child has trouble sitting still or is unable to concentrate on school work it may be that he or she may be feeling anxious. If this general restlessness has always been a part of your child's make-up, then it will probably be heightened by the divorce. If prior to the divorce, however, your child was calm but now is very restless, you can be fairly confident that the divorce situation has caused this anxiety.

COMBINATION OF REACTIONS

Most children will show more than one of these emotional responses during the first year or year and a half following their parents' separation. One child may be primarily sad, but have some anxiety as demonstrated by bad dreams and headaches after visitations. Another child may be very angry, getting into lots of fights at school and breaking windows in the neighborhood. This same child may also show sadness by breaking down and crying when told the judge has signed the final divorce papers.

If a child is always angry, the anger may be masking intense sadness. Such a child will need to be helped, but not forced, to express sadness. Conversely, if a child is always sad he or she may need some help in expressing anger in order to avoid depression. Expressing in a safe and constructive manner the natural anger and sadness related to the divorce will help the child in making a healthy adjustment.

NO OBSERVABLE RESPONSE

A few children may exhibit none of the responses described. These children appear somewhat detached from the divorce process, stating that "Nothing is really different." Or the child may even seem artificially cheerful, proclaiming "Everything is just great." These children will say that they have no questions about the divorce. They claim it is just something that happened and there is no need to think or feel about it.

This type of response in children is a special cause for concern. It could mean they have been exposed to so many intense emotions of others that they are afraid to have any feelings of their own. They might feel that "If my parents are out of control, I must remain in control." A lack of response could also mean that they are afraid of taking sides between their parents. To remain "faithful" to both parents, children sometimes decide to know and feel nothing. Finally, this reaction could mean that children are so devastated by the divorce that the resulting feelings seem unmanageable and overwhelming. As a result, they admit no feeling whatsoever.

If your child has not expressed any emotions or reactions to the divorce, you need to explore the possible reasons. It is important for you to take the time and effort necessary to create an atmosphere where it will be safe to "feel."

* * *

EXERCISE 6

Understanding Your Child's
Upside-Down World

FOR YOU

Dig out an old photograph of yourself as a grade-schooler—preferably one with your parents. Try to remember how you thought and acted then. Now imagine that your parents suddenly announced that they were divorcing. (If perchance your parents did in fact divorce or if one or both of them died when you were that age, then you will be able to do this exercise for real.)

Take a piece of paper and label it "How I Would Have Felt and Acted If My Parents Had Done This To Me." In one column write how you would have felt. Next to it write what actions you might have taken.

(GREG'S EXAMPLE)
HOW I WOULD HAVE FELT AND ACTED
IF MY PARENTS HAD DONE THIS TO ME

FELT	ACTED
1. Surprised.	a. Denied it to my friends.
	b. Kept thinking they would get back together.
2. Sad	a. Cried every night.
	b. Refused to go see non-custodial parent.
3. Sick	a. Threw up.
	b. Died.

Greg has been divorced twice himself. His own parents, however, have celebrated their fortieth wedding anniversary and are still living. It had never even occurred to Greg to think about how he would have felt as a child if his parents had divorced. The idea was so foreign to him that he thought he would have either vomited or even died if it had happened.

Just going through the exercise made Greg a lot more sensitive to how his own children must have felt when he and his wife divorced. It made him more understanding of the various ways his children had been acting out after his divorce and more determined to discover their true feelings.

The feeling children experience related to parental divorce are extremely varied and will continue to emerge over time. A single exercise may not provide enough opportunity for your child to express all of his or her feelings. Therefore, in addition to the specific exercises for each age group, there are also listed two general methods that you might use with any age children to help them express feelings about divorce.

EXERCISE FOR AGES 6-8

Children love stories. In story telling, aspects of an emotional struggle can be faced indirectly. This is a helpful way for children to deal with their feelings without making themselves too vulnerable.

Your child can tell you a brief story about anything. If he or she can't think of anything, you can start the story by saying, "Once upon a time, there was a little prince (or princess) who was feeling worried (angry, etc.) . . . Then let the child finish the story.

Sometimes the child will tell a story with little emotional significance. This is fine. Every exercise you do together does not need to be directly related to the divorce. By encouraging your child to tell a story, you have helped stimulate creativity and imagination. This is an exercise which can be repeated often. If your child enjoys telling you stories, eventually those stories will reveal quite a bit about what the child is feeling about your divorce.

You too can be the story-teller. Make up a story that will deal with the main concern you feel your child is expressing. For example, if the child is very fearful with Dad gone, you might tell a story of an Indian boy whose father was gone on a long hunt. Describe how the boy began to get afraid of noises at night and wanted to sleep with the mother. The Indian mother was wise and realized that the boy was afraid when the father was gone. She gave her son one of his father's belts to wear at night, telling him that this would make him brave like his father. During the day, she let the boy do a few more grown-up activities, like fishing.

Soon the boy was no longer afraid at night.

In this example, divorce is never mentioned, but the major emotional struggle the child was experiencing was transferred to another situation. In the story, there was a working through of the problem. No explanations are needed with these types of stories. Just hearing them will help a child work through similar problems.

EXERCISE FOR AGES 9-11

You will need paper and pen or pencil and several envelopes and stamps. This will be a letter writing exercise for your child.

Children are often able to express some of their feeling in writing when they cannot verbalize them. Tell you child that there are many grownups and children who might want to know how he or she feels about divorce. Suggest that the child might want to write to the judge, your attorney, a special teacher, a grandparent or aunt or uncle, a close adult friend or even you or your former spouse.

Ask your child to pick one or more of these people to write to. Tell him or her that the letter doesn't have to be mailed unless the child wants to, nor does the child have to show the letter to you. That way the child knows that he or she can be as honest as possible.

Some children may enjoy this experience very much and want to write several letters. Great! Let him or her express feelings about divorce. The adults who get the letters need to know how divorce is affecting your children. They can handle whatever your child writes.

Other children will find this a very emotional and difficult task. You may even observe the child acting out the very emotions he or she is trying to write about. It is very important that you be very sensitive and available to your child during this exercise. If he or she chooses to share the letter or letters with you, you need to spend time talking and listening together.

ADDITIONAL EXERCISES FOR ALL CHILDREN

1. Talking it out.

Begin by identifying a major response to the divorce—such as anger or fear—in your child. When you and your child are in a quiet place (riding alone in the car often presents a good opportunity), introduce the area of concern. You might say, "Are you feeling worried that I might leave you too?" Many times a child will say "no." In spite of the negative response, you might have just helped your child identify the feeling.

After your child has responded, it is important to assure him or her that it is normal under these circumstances to have these feelings. You may say, "The reason I thought you might be angry at me is that if my mother and father had gotten a divorce when I was your age I think I would have been angry. Even though I made the decision to file for divorce, I sometimes feel angry when I can't be home with you after school. I think Dad (or Mom) must be angry because he (or she) can't see you every day. So this is a time when we are all feeling angry."

What you have done is to identify the feeling, and then helped the child understand the appropriateness of such a feeling. Even if the child does not say much, this type of dialogue is very helpful. If you have more than one child there can be some family discussions related to feelings. It is extremely helpful, however, to talk with each child individually from time to time.

2. Do some physical activity together.

During this period of change and adjustment, promote a lot of physical activity in both your children and yourself. It is much better for everyone to not just sit and think but to engage in "doing something." Engaging in activities that use physical energy will help everyone ventilate some inner tension in non-destructive ways. Examples of things that would be helpful are running, swimming, roller skating, playing ball, skiing, going for a walk, or dancing.

Physical activity will not resolve the emotional struggles your children are experiencing, but it will reduce internal stress for a period of time. Doing the activity with you will help strengthen the bond between parent and child and will allow time to be together without "having" to talk. Immediately after doing one of the other exercises listed in this book is often a good time to try some strenuous activity together.

These two exercises may be varied and repeated over and over, for the emotional reactions of each child will change over time. Be sure a child is not feeling pressured into talking about the divorce more than is helpful. Allow some time to pass—a week or two at least—between the non-physical exercises. Physical exercise can be done whenever possible.

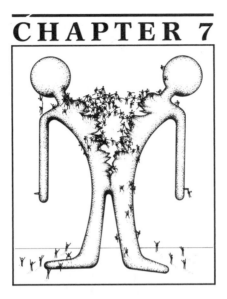

CHAPTER 7

VISITATION, CHILD SUPPORT, ETC.

"Kenny wants to go with me to his grandmother's for Easter, not to Florida with his father."

Pat, a divorced mother.

"Kenny is excited about going to Florida on his spring break, he has told me he can hardly wait."

Alan, a divorced father.

"Kenny, what do you want to do?"

Sara, the family's counselor.

Quietly, "I don''t know."

Kenny, their eight year old son.

For many parents, the process of divorce is never complete. It continues for a lifetime over issues relating to the children—the only cord still linking the couple. After a divorce is finalized, former spouses supposedly have nothing left to fight about. They, their lawyers, and finally a judge have created in the final decree the rules and guidelines for the division of properties and for the care of the children. The divorce decree guidelines are to be adhered to by both parties and were designed so that each parent's right to spend time with the child has been protected.

Many people, however, cannot "let go" of the conflict they have been engaged in during their marriage and the divorce process. They continue to fight, primarily over issues related to the children. Some decide they do not agree with the divorce decree and openly defy it. Some hold that the final decree was vague and continue to fight over interpretation. In many cases, new circumstances arise that were not covered in the decree, which leads to new fights. None of this is helpful to their children. Parents fight, fight, fight. . .and the children listen, observe and become increasingly anxious.

Kenny's parents are continuing their marital fighting long after their divorce has been finalized. Kenny's father, Alan, had a bad temper when he was married to Pat. He often demanded things be done his way, and if Pat had other ideas he would become angry, often breaking things around the home and then storming off. Eventually they divorced. Pat has custody of eight year old Kenny. The divorce decree, however, was vague when it came to specifying the guidelines for visitations: "reasonable and prearranged-upon visitations" was the wording. Pat, who felt put down and controlled by Alan for years, now has power. She will almost never agree to anything Alan requests. Kenny can't visit his father on weekends because he has Cub Scouts; he can't talk on the phone because he is in the bath tub; he can't go on vacation because they already have plans.

Alan is still struggling with his temper, but he wants to maintain a relationship with Kenny. . .and Kenny enjoys being with his father, although he is afraid to tell this to his mother. Although Pat has a meaningful job and some new friends, she has not let go of her former marital relationship. Her anger at Alan is always simmering just below the surface, and since she has been given so much authority in the divorce decree she is using it to punish Alan and to show him that she is now in charge. Kenny is the real one who is suffering.

After divorce a period of time is needed to heal all of the wounds and losses. During this time each former partner will begin to build a new life. One of the emotional tasks during this time is to let go of the marital role—being a spouse—but to maintain the role of being a parent. It may be difficult to co-parent with someone to whom you are no longer married and with whom you may feel very angry. Your ability and willingness to co-parent, however, is critical in helping your children during this period of adjustment.

Some divorced parents are able to make this transition very well. Joanne and Gene are such a couple. After ten years of marriage and two daughters, Vicky and Amy, ages eight and five, Gene fell in love with a woman in his office. Joanne was shocked, angry, and depressed. Before they finally divorced, the couple had several emotional scenes—in front of both their children and their lawyers. Finally, however, they worked out an agreement and the divorce was finalized.

Joanne has custody of Vicky and Amy, and Gene sees the girls every other weekend, a month in the summer, and various specified holidays. Joanne got a job as a teacher in the local high school and has found the job stimulating and time-consuming. She went back to graduate school in the evenings and has begun to date. Her life as a single person has flourished because she decided not to get stuck in her anger at Gene.

Gene lives in a high rise condominium with his new wife, Kay. He picks up the girls every other weekend, he calls them once or twice a week just to chat, and he attends parent-teacher conferences when he is in town. Joanne is still angry at Gene and she does not want to talk to Kay unless it is absolutely necessary, but she does not want her hurt to interfere in the girls' relationship with their father.

The results of their parents attitudes show in Vicky and Amy. They are well-adjusted, love both of their parents and exhibit few of the negative feelings about themselves shown by many other children of divorced parents.

For a variety of reasons, some parents are not as cooperative and mature as Joanne and Gene and thus continue to experience conflict around a number of issues. Arguments about child visitation, however, are at the center of most post-decree disagreements. There is a current trend to award joint custody to parents. This means that each parent has the right to have input into child rearing, and in these cases the children usually spend a considerable amount of time with each parent. In most instances, judges only award joint custody of the children to those parents who have a workable, sensible plan for the rearing of the children. Therefore, visitation should not be an issue for parents with joint custody.

Because they cannot get along, many divorcing parents are unable to work out a joint custody arrangement. Mothers are still awarded sole custody in almost 90% of divorces with minor children, a fact which frustrates and angers many divorcing fathers. When mother or father is awarded sole custody of the children, a plan to guarantee the other parent the right to spend time with the children must be worked out.

CONSIDERATIONS FOR BOTH PARENTS

If at all possible, children need to know and be cared for by both parents. Children want to love and respect each of their parents. Understanding and applying this principle will do more to help your children facilitate a healthy adjustment to your divorce than *anything* else you can do. You can probably think of a dozen reasons why your former spouse does not deserve to be respected and liked . . . look at the way he or she treated you! The less you push this view on your children, however, the better able they will be to form an independent evaluation of the other parent. If your former spouse really has despicable characteristics, your children will eventually learn about them firsthand and therefore will be less likely to blame you for them.

This does not mean you must defend your former spouse or paint an artificially positive picture of him or her. There is no point in pretending to like someone you do not! Be honest about your own feelings with your children and share with them the events that led to the end of your marriage. Do not, however, go on and on venting your feelings and opinions when a child is neither requesting nor desiring such input.

The very reasons a marriage breaks up may continue to be the core of the problems in post-divorce interaction between parents. Review the reasons you divorced. The same conflicts that resulted in divorce might very well be now creating these conflicts.

Terry and Anita divorced because they were very different psychologically and also had differences in values and beliefs. Anita valued freedom of expression and had a very relaxed, laissez-faire approach to life and parenting. If something didn't get done today, she would think about it tomorrow. Terry wanted more control of life, including the way they raised their child. He placed much importance on cleanliness.

Terry received custody of the couple's only son, Scott, primarily because Anita felt it would be better for a boy to be with his father. She believed that she and Terry could work out flexible visitations. Now that Terry has custody, however, he has become increasingly critical of Anita. He doesn't want Scott to visit her if her apartment isn't up to his standard of cleanliness. He grills Scott after visitations to find out the condition of the bathroom and the kitchen floor. If Anita is an hour late bringing Scott home, Terry is very angry. Scott can talk to Anita about many topics and has the freedom to disagree with her. Terry feels this is inappropriate behavior for Scott, and he wants Anita to change her style of parenting.

The very reasons Anita and Terry divorced are now creating difficulties in post divorce co-parenting. Terry still wants to control how Anita lives and is putting Scott in the center of their conflict.

To have a successful co-parenting relationship, one that is healthy for the children, each parent must allow the other the freedom to parent in his or her own way. You should interfere or raise objections to what the other parent is doing *only* if your child's physical or emotional well-being is threatened. If your child is being left alone for long periods, abused in some way, or exposed to sex, drugs or alcohol in a totally inappropriate way, then deal with that specific situation legally, under the provisions of the divorce decree. Otherwise, you must look the other way while your child is with your former spouse and hope that your values will be transmitted to your child through your words and actions while you are together.

In most post-divorce squabbles, the children's welfare is not being truly threatened—except from the stress engendered from being involved in ongoing bitter parental conflicts. If children sleep in a sleeping bag for a weekend or eat peanut butter for dinner, their safety is not jeopardized. If they miss church or stay up until midnight on Saturday night, their future is not at risk. If a child is required to dress up (or down) when visiting the other parent, it will cause no permanent damage. If children occasionally have to miss an extended-family party because they are with their other parent, no one is going to die. These examples may include some practices which you do not approve; it is certainly all right not to approve or like what the other parent does. You are probably divorced *because* you didn't agree on many issues and ideas. You do *not* however, have a right to try and control what your children do with the other parent. In divorce, both parents loose some control of parenting. If you can accept this fact, you will create a better emotional atmosphere for both yourself and your children.

SUGGESTIONS FOR CUSTODIAL PARENTS

1. **Your child needs to have consistent, stress-free visitations with the other parent.**

You have no power to control what happens when your child spends time with the other parent. Your attitude toward these visits, however, both before your children go and after they return, can influence the emotional tone of the visits. If your former spouse is thirty minutes late you can take off in the car with your child to "show him that he can't push us around," or you can wait patiently and when he does show up send your child off with a hug, accepting the explanation that your former spouse was tied up in a traffic jam. (If a pattern develops in which your former spouse is being truly and objectively irresponsible, deal directly with him or her—but not when the children are around.)

If you have developed the habit of trying to undermine and interfere with visitations, it is you who is creating stress for your children. You can buy tickets for a special baseball game on your former spouse's weekend with the children, knowing it will cause problems; or you can plan such special outings only for those weekends you have your children with you. You can take your vacation at exactly the same time as your former spouse, or you can work to coordinate summer vacations for the maximum benefit of your children.

Children hear the two of you arguing on the phone. They observes you slamming the door or changing plans at the last minute. The message you send to your child is, "I hate your Dad (or your Mom)." Your children will be hurt by this and will withdraw from being honest with you. They will begin to tell you only what you want to hear or will become openly angry at you. Neither of these reactions are very productive for them or for you.

Many parents say something like this: "But Tricia doesn't want to go visit her Dad (or Mom). She has all her friends and toys here. Why should she have to go when she doesn't want to?" In many cases, this is merely a projection of the parent's feeling onto the child. Some parents, however, legitimately wonder how much influence a child's opinion should have over visitations. Taking a child's wishes and desires into account may complicate the planning of visitations. If both parents and their children have non-hostile and open communications, visitations can be varied to meet changes in either parent's schedule or to accommodate specific desires of the child. Frequently, however, such open communication does not exist. In these cases, visitation schedules should be strictly adhered to. Younger children especially will respond to a little bit of rigidity better than a lot of tension over each visit. As children approach adolescence, they can communicate more directly with the non-custodial parent and make appropriate adjustments to visitations.

A final note of warning to custodial parents. Both you and your former spouse have had to make adjustments to accommodate visitations; so will your child. Being a child from a divorced family is *not* like being a child from an intact family. It is important for children to recognize and accept their responsibility for communicating their desires to the non-custodial parent. If you are constantly raising the visitation issue, then it will be unclear whether it is you or the child who is questioning the present arrangement.

2. You cannot force the other parent to exercise visitation rights.

In most instances, the non-custodial parent wants very much to maintain a relationship with his or her child. There are some cases, however, where a parent deserts the family or when a parent will not or cannot maintain contact with the child. This lack of contact may be the result of a number of factors: progressive alcoholism, guilt over the divorce, or the inability to really care for another person. If that has happened to your children it may be very sad for both you and them, especially since you know how important it is for your child to know and care for the other parent. In spite of your feelings there is *nothing* you can do to change your former spouse, and you certainly cannot force him or her to see the child.

You *can* answer your child's questions honestly and tell your child about the other parent. Share how you met, why you loved each other, and why you believe visitations are not occurring. This knowledge might help your child accept the parental rejection, and it will also reassure them that the rejection did not come about because they were "bad" or "unloveable."

SUGGESTIONS FOR NON-CUSTODIAL PARENTS

1. Your child needs your consistent attention and concern.

You are now in the difficult position of having a child that needs you but does not live with you. It is probably a position you are not too happy about. Some non-custodial parents, experiencing so much pain in seeing their child only occasionally and in watching their relationship becoming fragmented, stop visiting with the child altogether. This can have disastrous consequences for a child. It is extremely important for the healthy development of children that if at all possible they relate to both parents on a regular, dependable basis. The fact that the effort to relate with your children is more difficult after a divorce is not an acceptable excuse for not filling this basic need.

Consistency is the crucial feature of the visitations with your child. If you see your child every other weekend and for two weeks in the summer, then make sure you show up every other weekend. If you live across the country and only see your child during Christmas vacation and in the summer, then call your child every week or two at a specific time, send post cards and notes, and be *sure* to arrange the extended visits. After a year or two of consistent contact with you, your child will become reassured that you will be there for him or her. *Telling* a child you will always be available is not the same as *showing* that you will be there.

Most non-custodial parents are fathers. Professionals who study the development of children are discovering that fathers play a very important role in the development of a child's self-esteem. Children who admire and have positive contact with their fathers, for example, are better achievers in school than children who have little or negative contact with their fathers. These findings underscore the need for your ongoing input of time and concern to your developing children. They need more from you than just money.

There may be times when you do not feel like making the effort to see your child. Perhaps your former spouse makes arranging visitations very difficult, or the last time you were with your child you felt the child seemed bored, or your new girlfriend (boyfriend) or spouse does not like sharing you with your child. In spite of these or a myriad of other reasons, please go ahead with the visits as planned. Keep at it; you will realize much later how important it is.

2. Don't expect too much immediate gratification from your children.

Non-custodial parents sometimes make the mistake of expecting too much emotional support and recognition from their children. They are then disappointed when they feel their child has let them down. A school age child's main concerns and thoughts are focused on the immediate environment; thus your child will be concerned about what is on T.V., whom to ask over to play, and if there are Frosted Flakes in the house. Your child will probably not be thinking about calling Dad or Mom to share the results of the unit spelling test, or remembering to send a Valentine or Halloween card. Your birthday and holidays may go unnoticed. Do not take this personally. Remember that any child needs help and encouragement in remembering these events. If your former spouse is unwilling to help your child to remember your special occasions, accept this with as much good grace as you can muster. When your child becomes older you can expect him or her to become more considerate. (On the reverse side, do you remind your children to remember your former spouse's birthday, etc?)

Keep sending cards and presents and get-well notes to your child. You are setting an example of how to care for someone when they are far away. This is an important lesson for your child to learn: that you can think about, care for, and love another person even if you don't live with them.

A non-custodial parent must put a lot of energy into the long range goal of the development of an emotionally healthy child and the creation of a good parent-child relationship. Considerable time and thoughtfulness is required of you now, and much of the pay-off will not come for years. Of course there are many joys you will experience in spending time with your children as they grow, but the most important satisfaction you will have is in knowing you have contributed substantially to your child's development.

CHILDREN'S REACTIONS TO VISITATIONS

There is a process that most children go through when they go to visit a non-custodial parent. Understanding this process will help you understand your child. A few days or the day before the visitation, a child may begin to come up with reasons why he or she doesn't want to go: "I'm going to miss you," or "It's no fun at Mom's (or Dad's)." or "I don't want to be away from my kitten." All of these reasons are partially true, but they are also a protesting against leaving the security of a known environment.

When a child is picked up by Dad or Mom, he or she may be fairly quiet. The two of them need some time to begin to feel comfortable together again. In the middle of the visitation there is usually a period of time where both the non-custodial parent and the child feel very close and natural. This is the best part of many visitations, a little slice of time when neither parent or child is emotionally coping with loss and thus can be open and spontaneous.

As the visitation starts to draw to an end, children realize it will soon be time to leave again. They often begin to withdraw from the non-custodial parent and may show signs of sadness about going home. This sadness can take many different forms. When they arrive back home, they may be angry, hyperactive, or

78

withdrawn for a period of time. The custodial parent sometimes believes that this is because of "things my ex-husband (or ex-wife) put in their head." Although that is always a possibility, it is more likely the children's expression—through behavior—of all the feelings associated with having to leave one parent, get close to the other parent, then leave that parent, and get close to the first one all over again. Think about how you would feel in such an arrangement!

Visitations call for many and sometimes rapid adjustments, regardless of the length of time of the visitation—whether a two hour dinner or a two month summer stay the process remains the same. Grade school age children are usually not conscious of this emotional pattern and do not understand why they are feeling so upset. The older children become, the better able they are to understand and cope with these emotional responses; but the cycle remains the same no matter how old they are.

This emotional closeness and then separation often drives the non-custodial parent crazy. If a visitation is very short—two hours for example—the period of closeness may be extremely brief, perhaps only five to ten minutes. The non-custodial parent may begin to question if the child even cares for him or her and wonder if visitations are worth the effort.

The custodial parent may also misunderstand the emotional cycle of visitations. Some custodial parents buy into the child's expression of not wanting to go and try to interrupt or stop visitations. They often become angry at the child and non-custodial parent when the child exhibits worrisome behavior upon returning home.

One excellent way parents can help children deal with visitation is to verbalize what the children may be feeling. Before the visitation, for example, the custodial parent might say, "I know that you will miss Fluffy and me, but you will have a good time with Dad (or Mom). I will be here Monday night when you get back, and you can always call me." By doing this you are reassuring your children that you will not desert them and also reinforcing the positive aspects of visiting the other parent.

A non-custodial parent could say, "I'm feeling sad that our visit is almost over, it sure has gone fast for me. Tomorrow I will take you home to Mom's (or Dad's), and even though I will miss you I will call you next week and then we'll be together again next month." You are expressing your own feelings about the visitation ending but also providing a positive reinforcement about returning home and giving each of you something to anticipate.

Finally, if a child appears upset about returning home, the custodial parent might say, "I know you miss Dad (or Mom) and feel angry about this divorce. Would you like to call him (or her) tomorrow night?" Such comments validate a child's feelings, which will help ease the return home.

It is very natural for both parents to resent all the emotional energy spent on seeing that visitations go smoothly. It is especially difficult when after a visitation a child appears angry and upset. Carol, a divorced mother of six, shared her feelings about visitation: "Who needs this? I am trying to be the 'good guy' by being cooperative, supportive, and understanding, and what do I get in return? Angry children and a non-appreciative former spouse!"

All parties—both parents and all children—have to make some adjustments to facilitate visitations. It is worth the effort. In time it will become easier for everyone to make the changes necessary for them to succeed.

CHILD SUPPORT

The divorce decree establishes an amount of money the non-custodial parent (usually the father) is required to pay the custodial parent to help support the child. This is generally an amount agreed upon by the parties. Where the parties are unable to agree the amount is fixed by the court. After the divorce the easiest way to avoid conflict in this area is for the non-custodial parent to pay the required amount in a timely fashion. A good record of child support payments tends to reduce conflict.

If you are the non-custodial parent, it is critical to keep in mind that the money is helping provide a secure home for your children. You also must accept the fact that you can not dictate how the money is to be spent. The money is given to the custodial parent to use as needed. If you remarry or incur other financial responsibilities after the divorce, *this does not reduce your responsibility to your children.* If your income drops, substantially affecting your ability to pay, speak to an attorney to help modify the amount. Do not stop or reduce payment without seeking legal advice.

When the child support check comes late or not at all it can create an upsetting situation not only for the custodial parent but for the children as well. This money if often necessary to pay for essential living expenses, such as rent, food, utilities and clothing. When a person fails to meet these obligations, bill collectors may begin to call and utility services can be shut off. This type of financial crisis creates tension, worry, and embarrassment for children. In addition to feeling worried, they may feel angry at both parents for failing to care for them.

Money is often used by people to control others. Withholding child support or demanding more child support may be a way of trying to get at your former spouse. If you are having conflicts over child support, try to determine what really is behind the conflict. Are you trying to manipulate your former spouse? Do you resent paying money and having no say over the spending?

It is normal if you are paying child support to be incensed if there is little or no recognition from your former spouse or your children about the child support money. Paying child support, however, is another cost of divorce. To be at peace with yourself, you need to gradually become reconciled with this obligation—whether the support is recognized or not.

There are cases in which the custodial parent will request an increase in child support or the non-payment of child support continues to be an issue. In these situations, both parents must avoid involving the children in their continuing legal controversy. Children usually know something is going on, however, and should be told the truth if they ask about the problem. In no case should the children be made to feel that they have caused the problem. A parent might tell a child: "Mom (or Dad) and I disagree about the amount of child support, and a judge will need to decide since we both think that we're right."

After a decision on child support has been made, unless unusual circumstances exist neither side should continue the legal battle. For the sake of the children, both the custodial and the non-custodial parent should accept the decision of the court. Ongoing legal fighting drains everyone, especially your children.

MEDICAL FEES

In addition to visitation procedures and child support payments, divorce decrees often contain provisions relating to the child's medical care—including how decisions are made regarding recommended treatment and the payment for medical services. Frequently the father is to provide medical insurance for the child and pay for extraordinary health expenses not covered by insurance. The mother is generally then required to pay for so called "routine" medical expenses, which are often defined in terms of a fixed sum of money to be paid for each medical occurrence. For example, the first $25 may be deemed to be routine expenses. The agreements virtually always provide that the father is to be consulted prior to the administration any medical treatment, except were the child's life might be imperiled by delay. This certainly sounds fair and straightforward.

Problems usually arise when either parent does not follow the terms of the decree, assuming the right to ignore or misinterpret the guidelines. For example, if a child is to have elective surgery—say the removal of moles, a non-emergency appendectomy, or any cosmetic surgery—some custodial parents assume that they have the authority of schedule the surgery without including the non-custodial parent in the process and that by "informing" the parent of the surgery they have complied with the terms of the decree. Merely informing the non-custodial parent of planned surgery does not meet the requirements of "prior consultation," which implies being involved in the decision-making process. Non-custodial parents can cause conflict over medical procedures when they decide the custodial parent is taking the child to the doctors too often and arbitrarily decide not to pay for the services.

In each of these examples, parents tend to become very embroiled and angry. Children are often exposed to these disagreements and feel worried and upset. Have they caused this problem by being ill? This is an unfair burden for a child. In medical expenses above all else, follow the procedures in your divorce decree, respect your former spouse as an interested, caring parent, and relinquish the need to decide and control. For the sake of your children, try co-parenting.

REPORT CARDS

An issue over which divorced parents sometimes clash is the non-custodial parent's right to have a copy of the child's report card. Many school districts send only one report card home, to the custodial parent. If divorced parents cooperate in co-parenting, the custodial parent simply makes a photocopy of the report card and sends it to the other parent. If the custodial parent is uncooperative and wants to exercise control, however, he or she may refuse to send a copy of the report card and refuse to give the school permission to release any information to the non-custodial parent.

School administrators should be encouraged to institute policies and procedures which will insure that both parents will receive copies of the report cards and other important school information. School personnel are justifiably leery of involvement in the legal conflict between parents, but if school boards, in conjunction with their legal counsel, would begin to endorse the rights of both parents to parent, it would contribute to the elimination of several areas of conflicts between parents. In addition, it would be an acknowledgement of the existence of many divorced families by the schools. (Some areas now guarantee by law the non-custodial parent's right to his or her children's school records.)

* * *

The important consideration on all divorce related issues should always be what is best for the child. That will mean that both parents will give in or accommodate on issues over which they might like to "go to the mat" with their former spouses. Save "going to the mat" for issues which involve your child's actual physical or emotional safety.

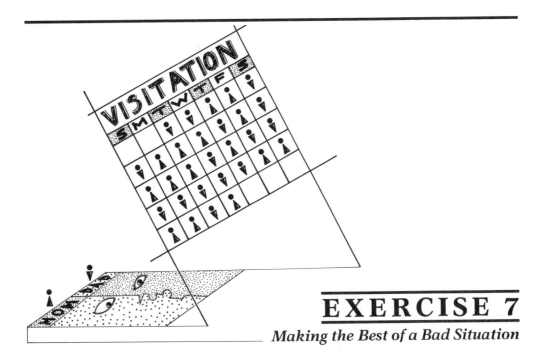

EXERCISE 7

Making the Best of a Bad Situation

FOR YOU

Across the top of a sheet of paper write "Visitations." Now divide your paper in to three columns: "Concerns," "Feelings" and "Possible Solutions." In the first column list all the concerns and worries you currently have about visitation, in the next column write down how that concern makes you feel, and in the last column use your creative mind to come up with possible solutions. Decide which of the solutions you will implement in the upcoming week.

(ALICE'S EXAMPLE)

VISITATIONS

CONCERNS	FEELINGS	POSSIBLE SOLUTIONS
1. Will Fred (former husband) take Kent and Carrie to his new girlfriend Sue's house. I don't want them there.	Anger, anxiety, and worry (that they will like her).	a. Talk to Fred rationally. Ask him to wait a month or two before the children meet Sue. Tell him how I feel. b. Accept the fact that Fred will be dating and the children will have to get used to it.

(continued)

83

2. Will Fred see that Kent takes his medicine?	Concern, worry, wishing Kent could be home with me when he is sick.	a. Write a note to Fred explaining the medicine.
		b. Tell Kent about the times he is to take medicine.
3. Will Fred give Carrie the Sunshine Doll that I can't afford?	Jealousy—wish I had Fred's income.	a. Buy her a Sunshine Doll myself, even if I have to charge it.
		b. Try to let go of my jealousy. If Carrie gets the doll, let her enjoy it.
		c. Try to improve my skills so that I can get a better job.
4. Will Kent and Carrie brush their teeth?	Concern.	a. Remind them to brush their teeth before they go.
		b. Send a note.
		c. Remember that not brushing one night will not damage their teeth permanently.

(COMMENT)

After Alice, a divorced mother of two, had completed this exercise, she discovered that her main concerns were worrying about things that had not yet happened. Some of her worries were related to still feeling hurt and and resentful toward her former husband Fred. Other worries were health related concerns about her children, Kent and Carrie, but she became aware that these concerns were not of a life and death nature.

Seeing her concerns in writing helped Alice begin to accept that she was divorced and there would be many times that the children would not be in her control. She also realized that it was difficult for her to let go of Fred. By accepting his independent relationship with the children, she was beginning to do so.

The following exercises designed to explore feeling and concerns related to visitations may be very "risky" for your children. You will be asking them to share positive (as well as negative) feelings about your former spouse and to expose negative (as well as positive) concerns that relate to you. Your children may worry about the ramifications of honestly expressing these concerns and feelings.

Will you get angry? Will you attempt to talk them out of their feelings? Will you use what is shared to hurt your former spouse? How you respond will be a critical factor affecting the future trust between you and your child. Do not get angry or become defensive. These are your children's feelings, and they will never see events—or feel about events—exactly as have you or your former spouse felt or experience events.

EXERCISES FOR AGES 6-8

You will need a small paper bag and about ten slips of paper. This game may be played over dinner or lunch. If you have more than one child, including older children, encourage everyone to play. Be sure, however, that a younger child is heard and allowed the time needed to express himself or herself.

On each slip of paper write a partially completed statement related to visitations, with a blank at the end of the statement. For example, "My favorite thing to eat at Dad's (or Mom's) house is _____," or "When I am packing to go to Mom's (or Dad's) I feel _____," or "The best thing about my room at my other home is _____."

Have each child pick a slip of paper, read it, and fill in the blank. You should play, too, changing the situation to how you feel when your children packs to leave or a mentioning a special treat you eat when they are gone. This game often triggers interesting family talks.

EXERCISE FOR AGES 9-11

Take out a large piece of plain paper. Divide the paper in half and write "Mom" as the heading for one column and "Dad" as the heading for the other.

Ask your child to list all things he or she likes about Mom's house and all the good things about Dad's house. If your child can't think of anything you might encourage him or her to consider special food or television shows shared at each home. ("Doesn't yell" and "Lets me stay up late" are two all-time favorites.)

After your child has listed some positive qualities ask him or her to write down the things not liked about "Dad's" and "Mom's." Be sure to encourage as many negative items about your own home as about your former spouse's.

This exercise for your child may have several important functions. It was designed to give your child permission to acknowledge there are good things about the other parent's home and visitation and to allow an expression of negative aspects about your home. It will demonstrate very specifically the ambivalence of post-divorce life for the child—that there are good and not so good factors. Finally, it may spark a conversation with your child about his or her visitation concerns.

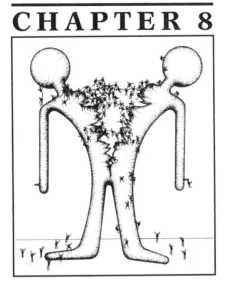

CHAPTER 8

GRANDPARENTS, AUNTS, UNCLES AND ADULT FRIENDS

"Since Stan and I separated his parents never call me, or even Michelle. I used to talk to his mother on the phone at least once a week, and they would stop by when they were out shopping. Now Michelle only sees them when Stan takes her to their house, which isn't very often."

Anna, a divorced mother.

Anna shared this observation while discussing her options in planning her eleven year old daughter Michelle's birthday party. Stan and Anna had been separated for eight months, and their divorce had been final for only six weeks. Before they separated, Stan's parents had played an important part in the family: together they celebrated all holidays and everyone's birthday.

Anna and Stan usually communicate quite well, especially when it concerns Michelle. Anna has custody of Michelle, but Stan still makes time for her. Stan's parents, Michelle's grandparents, however, had dropped out of the family scene.

The adjustment to divorce is a very complicated process, even when it is limited to the divorcing parents and their children. Yet a family that divorces does not exist in a vacuum. There are usually relatives and other significant people who have close relationships with the parents and children. Reaction to the divorce by others close to the family may effect the post-divorce adjustment of all family members.

Relationships with grandparents, aunts, uncles, cousins and adult family friends may become unclear and strained following a divorce. Extended family members frequently agonize over their problems in interacting with a divorced family. Likewise, after a divorce both parents and children may not know how to act toward relatives, former friends and in-laws.

With a little bit of work, however, those who were important to you and your children prior to the divorce may willingly continue to be supportive resources and loving relationships.

GRANDPARENTS

After Anna and Stan separated, his mother stopped calling Anna. Anna called once or twice after the separation but when she picked up on the older woman's uneasiness, she gave up. Anna thought perhaps Stan's parents were angry and were blaming her for the divorce. She felt badly about the loss of contact with her former in-laws, for her own parents lived 1,200 miles away. Anna felt even worse for her in-laws than she did for herself. The retired couple had enjoyed Michelle, and now they seldom saw her.

With Anna's permission, a counselor she was seeing phoned Stan and asked if he would be willing to bring his parents to a session to talk about whether they would like to see more of Michelle. He agreed to ask them. His parents were leery of counselors, and so it was with some reluctance that they agreed to meet.

Stan's parents are like many grandparents. They grew up in an era where divorce was uncommon. Both are devout Catholics and were having a very difficult time accepting the fact that their oldest son was divorced. It became clear that they were as uneasy with their own son, Stan, as they were with Anna. They felt ashamed of having a divorce in the family. They had not even told some relatives that Stan and Anna were divorced. They felt that their son's divorce somehow reflected on the kind of parents they had been. Had they raised Stan wrong?

The counselor acknowledged their concerns and helped them understand that Stan and Anna's divorce was a decision made by two responsible adults and that they had not raised a bad son. They saw how Stan was meeting his financial responsibilities to Anna and Michelle and how he faithfully spent time with his daughter. Stan was also willing to begin the official church annulment process, which seemed to relieve his mother. They were urged to discuss some of their concerns with a priest they admired and respected. By this time in the conversation, the elderly couple was more relaxed and began talking about Michelle. They too missed seeing her and Anna, and when told that Anna and Michelle missed them too the grandfather began to cry. In no time at all a plan was worked out where they would pick up Michelle once a month on a Saturday night. The little girl would sleep over with her grandparents, attend Mass with them, go out for Sunday brunch and then Anna would pick her up.

Both grandparents said they would love to have Anna come into their home to visit for a while when she picked up Michelle. They also wanted to continue to see Michelle in school programs, and were happy to be given "official" permission to continue a relationship with Michelle and Anna that did not always have to include Stan.

This particular story had a happy ending, but in many instances the results are not as happy. Some divorced people do not like their former in-laws, some even blame them for the divorce. Some grandparents become so embroiled in the divorce process that they even become embittered toward their own grandchildren.

There exist no socially accepted rules for how parents should act when their adult children divorce. Very few divorce decrees deal with the rights of the grandparents. If their divorced son or daughter does not arrange for them to have contact, these unhappy victims of the divorce often feel they have no effective means to maintain a relationship with their grandchildren. Many grandparents simply don't know what to do. They feel stigmatized, confused and embarrassed. As a result they may withdraw from your family.

If at all possible, children need to know (or know about) their grandparents in order to have a real sense of their identity and "roots." When two people divorce, they are no longer legally connected to each other. Their children, however, will always be biologically, legally, and socially tied to both sides of their heritage.

The importance of grandparents to their grandchildren has begun to be recognized by the legal community in the granting of legal visitation rights to grandparents. The State of Illinois divorce act, for example, was recently amended to provide that grandparents may petition the court and secure an order granting them the right to visitation with their grandchildren. The action by the legislature is in response to the important role that grandparents can play in the welfare of the children. In a number of cases the custody of the children has even been awarded to the grandparents.

You do not need to take on all the responsibility for maintaining your children's relationship with your former spouse's parents. You are younger and more flexible than the grandparents, however, and your actions might encourage initial contacts. Here are some suggestions for promoting a good post-divorce relationship:

- Communicate directly with your former in-laws. Tell them you hope they will continue to see the children. Work out a plan that is mutually agreeable.

- Do not discuss the divorce or their son or daughter's behavior, as this may cause tension. Do not try to get them on your side, for most parents will support their own child. Any attempts at discrediting their child will only result in tension between you and the grandparents.

- Encourage your child to send cards to their grandparents at holidays and birthdays. School age children will usually not remember to do this on their own; they need your help in remembering.

- If your former in-laws live a long distance away, have the children write or call occasionally. Perhaps you too could write, telling about what the children are doing.

- Invite the grandparents to school occasions, ball games and dance recitals. Send school pictures; grandparents love those pictures!

Not only your parent-in-laws will have a problem with the divorce. What about your own parents? They may also have some difficulty in understanding and accepting your divorce. Tell your parents exactly what you and your children need from them. For example, you might say, "Dad and Mom, I know you don't really approve of our getting a divorce, but I hope you won't be angry at me and the children about it. Please understand that I am working very hard and trying to take care of the children alone. Sometimes I may just need to complain a little. It doesn't mean you have to solve my problems. Maybe you could take the children to the ball game or out to the driving range once in a while. They would like it, and it would give me a break."

Of course, asking for what you need doesn't guarantee that you will always get it. When grandparents (your parents) are specifically asked for support, however, they almost always come through for their child and grandchildren.

In the traumatic time of divorce, both adults and children need the love, support and interest of people who care for them. Grandparents often have time and resources to give. It is a nice exchange.

During one in-service workshop for approximately 150 teachers, I asked them to think of a child from a single parent home who was well-adjusted and doing well in school. Then I asked them to think about what it was about that child that seemed to contribute to this positive adjustment. One of the most important factors cited by the teachers was the involvement and support of at least one grandparent.

OTHER RELATIVES

If the status and role of grandparents in divorce is undefined and fuzzy, the role and rights of other relatives is non-existent. Prior to the divorce, your family may have frequently celebrated holidays with your wife's side of the family. She has several brothers and sisters, all married, several with children. At these occasions the little cousins would roughhouse or ride bikes, while the parents would marvel at how much the children had grown and exchange outgrown clothes. A favorite sister or brother was selected to be your child's godmother or godfather. Aunt and Uncle always sent special birthday and Christmas gifts to the children. This family ritual had continued for the eight years you had been married.

Now comes the divorce. What should you do about these people who have been so dear to you and your children? Your former spouse will most likely continue to see his or her relatives and take your children to see their aunts, uncles and cousins. If your former spouse is not keeping up with his or her relatives (for whatever reason), however, your children might be losing contact with people they love. And what about you? You really liked some of your spouse's relatives. Should you send cards at holidays, invite them to your home, send gifts to your nieces and nephews, make attempts to stay in touch?

There are no easy answers to these questions. The answers depend on the nature of your relationship with the extended family prior to the divorce, how much damage the divorce process did to those relationships, and the attitudes and wishes of the extended family.

If you had a genuine, warm and caring relationship with your former spouse's brothers and sisters, and if during the divorce they managed not to become embroiled in any major disagreements, then perhaps now you can cultivate and maintain a separate, but meaningful, relationship with them. You must remember, however, that they are your former spouse's relatives. If he or she is attempting to place emotional and physical distance between the two you, then in all likelihood you will not be invited to extended family functions. Do not take this personally. Understand the delicate position of your former relatives.

What you can do is create some new events to share. Perhaps when the children are with you a favorite aunt and uncle can be invited for pizza or cousins can be asked to a birthday sleep-over with your children. Send appropriate remembrances of birthdays and special events. This will be an acknowledgment of your feelings and will encourage building ongoing, supportive relationships for you and your child.

Aunts and uncles and cousins may not know what role they have in this new, split family. Like grandparents, they may withdraw and wait until you make a move by phoning or planning a get-together. Do not interpret the lack of initiative on their part as not caring. Think about the type of new relationship you want to structure and then reach out to them.

Creating a new family alignment may not be a real possibility for you. Perhaps you did not even like your former spouse's relatives prior to the divorce but tolerated them at family functions. They may have lived such a distance away that you really never got to know them. During the divorce, your spouse may have involved them to such an extent that you still harbor angry, hurt feelings. If any of these situations closely reflect your circumstances, it is best to accept this reality and not try to force artificial, strained get-togethers.

You can, however, help your children immensely by not speaking negatively about their aunts, uncles and cousins, and by understanding your child's need to have contact with and permission to enjoy extended families on both sides.

Bonnie, a divorced mother, has eight grown brothers and sisters all living within a ten mile radius of her home. Bonnie's former husband Frank resented the closeness of the extended family when he and Bonnie were married, as a result he never felt like he quite "fit in." During the divorce Bonnie's brothers and sisters were very supportive of her; they drove her to court, loaned her money, and took her and her children into their homes. This made Frank furious because he wanted Bonnie to need him so much that she would consider a reconciliation.

After the divorce when the children went to visit their father, Frank would constantly run down Bonnie's brothers and sisters—the children's aunts and uncles. The children loved their aunts and uncles, and they also loved their father. The more Frank talked about the aunts and uncles, the more the children withdrew from their father, finally reaching the point where they no longer wanted to visit him.

Understand the need of your children to feel proud of all of their family members, your side and your former spouse's side. You do not have to share your child's feelings, but you must not attempt to force your child to mirror your feelings.

FAMILY FRIENDS

Your child's relationships with close adult family friends may also be affected by the divorce. Relationships may be lost or altered when your children move away from the family residence or when adult friends are primarily "Mom's" or primarily "Dad's." After the divorce, these people seldom see the child if the child lives with the parent who is not their close friend.

Although loss of contact with adult friends may not be as hurtful as the loss of contact with relatives, it still represents change and discontinuity. More importantly, adult friends can be important sources of support to children. If there are adults who have been especially interested in your children, try to encourage the relationship to continue in some manner. For example, on Saturday afternoon make a visit to the old neighborhood to see an elderly neighbor, or allow your children to have an overnight "vacation" with the young couple who used to enjoy taking them to the movies.

If there was a friend of your former spouse who was close to your child, you may want to suggest acceptable ways for the relationship to continue. Telephone the friend and say, "Glen, you and my son Mike always enjoyed each other. Even though Don and I are divorced I hope you will continue to see Mike. Feel free to call him anytime. I would feel awkward having you visit him at my apartment, but he will be visiting Don ever other weekend and I know he would love to see you there." This is a very clear message to Glen. It tells him that Mike's mother values his input into her son's life and hopes it will continue. She also makes it clear that it would not be acceptable to visit Mike in her home.

If you do contact a friend of your former spouse be sure you limit your conversation to his or her relationship with your child and general topics not related to the divorce. Do not use this contact to try to glean information about your former spouse or to pass along information. That would be using your child's relationship as a manipulative ploy. Don't forget *your* friends either. Many of them would be willing to take a small part in helping to raise your children.

If, in your network of friends and relatives there are not enough role models for your children, you might want to investigate a social work agency such as Big Brothers or Big Sisters. These programs help provide adult friends for children who need them.

Over time, all relationships change. New friends are made, old ones fade away. For whatever reason, some adults may lose interest in your children. If during the first year or so following separation you can help your children maintain these meaningful relationships, however, it will help foster a sense of security. Your children and adult friends may need encouragement from you to accomplish this.

* * *

My former husband, Jerry, was an only child, and both of his parents were dead by the time we had been married two years. Thus over time my family became his family, they loved him and he loved them. When we divorced after seventeen years of marriage, it was difficult for everyone to sort out what type of relationships should continue. The relationships that have been maintained are based on the mutual respect and caring that had developed over the years. Jerry corresponds directly with my extended family, remembering birthdays and Christmas. My father, who likes to call his own children, also calls Jerry just to chat about his job and fishing. When my mother was in failing health, Jerry took vacation time and flew from San Francisco to Florida to spend several days visiting her . . . this was seven years after our divorce! I find that not only do these contacts *not* bother me, but that I am very glad that they have continued for both my former husband's sake and that of our children.

So, although family and friendship ties do change, they do not have to end. You do have a choice.

EXERCISE 8

Reconnecting the Broken Links

FOR YOU

Think about the adults who have meaningful relationships with each of your children. Consider especially your child's relationships with relatives . . . grandparents, aunts, and uncles. For this exercise choose one or two relationships that might be damaged or even lost as a result of changes since the divorce.

Divide a piece of paper into three columns. Write the name of each endangered relationship in the first column; in the center column write down why you believe the relationship is in jeopardy; and in the third column try to come up with ways to foster the continuance of the relationship.

(EMILY'S EXAMPLE)

ENDANGERED RELATIONSHIP	WHY?	WAYS TO HELP
1. John and Beth's relationship with Grandmother Andrews (my former husband, Nathan's mother. His father is dead).	a. Mrs. Andrews does not drive anymore, and she lives over 100 miles away.	a. Encourage the children to keep in contact with her. I don't have to very involved.
	b. Mrs. Andrews does not "believe" in divorce, and has not spoken to me since we divorced.	b. Allow Nathan to have an extra weekend three times a year to take the children to visit her.
	c. I do not like Mrs. Andrews very much.	c. Help the children pick out a little Christmas gift for her.
		d. Find an old picture of Nathan's mother and frame it for the children.
		e. Watch what I say about Mrs. Andrews.
2. Beth's relationship with Nathan's sister Ann, and her children, especially Tracy. Beth and Tracy are the same age and loved playing together.	a. Ann is working and doesn't have time to come get Beth.	a. Call Ann myself. We used to be close. I could take first step.
	b. Ann has not spoken to me since the divorce.	b. Ask Tracy to come visit Beth. Since I am working part-time, I could drive to pick her up after school.
	c. Nathan seldom visits Ann, so Beth probably won't visit Tracy when she visits her Dad.	c. Send Ann and her family a Thanksgiving card. That's the next holiday coming up.

(COMMENT)

Emily has two children, John and Beth. In doing this exercise, she realized that she really did not like her former mother-in-law, but that it would be good for her children to maintain contact with their grandmother.

One important insight that Emily gained was that she had to watch what she was saying about her children's grandmother. Emily also realized that her daughter had lost a good friend and playmate in her cousin, Tracy. Because her sister-in-law worked full-time, Emily realized that it was up to her to make the first move and to offer to do some of the driving.

Extended family members or adult friends can be potential assets or create problems for you and your children. The following exercises could strengthen such relationships. Start with those individuals with whom you feel would be most helpful for each child to keep in contact, then repeat the exercises with as many people as a child desires. You can repeat each exercise every month or two. If your children reach out to these people, most will reach back to them. Be open to their overtures.

EXERCISES FOR AGES 6-8

You will need a set of recent photos of your child, a map, paper, paste, envelopes and stamps.

Have each child make a card for their grandparents or godparents by pasting a recent school photo on a piece of paper and then writing a little message or just signing it. By seeing that your children do something thoughtful for these people, you are telling everyone that the relationship is important and that it is all right with you for it to continue.

When your children have finished, put the papers into envelopes and help your children address them. You might find the addressee's houses on a map, starting with where you live and showing your children where the letters will be going. Take a trip to the mailbox together, and on the way tell your children some things about the people they are writing and how important it is to keep in touch with them.

EXERCISES FOR AGES 9-11

You will need a box of old photographs, your telephone book and a telephone.

Have your child look through the photographs and find someone that they miss. Talk with your child about the person or people they picked, remembering good times you had together. Explain that because of the divorce, perhaps some people are embarrassed to contact the child and that maybe the child should take the first step.

Ask your child to make a brief call to each person identified. Young people at this age usually love to initiate telephone calls, especially if they are long distance. If it is appropriate, let the child arrange a visit at your house, the relative's or friend's house or at a restaurant.

If the relative or friend comes to your home, your child can help fix some simple refreshments, such as baking cookies the night before. Your child will enjoy the creative activity, and your participation will express an acceptance of how important this person is to your child.

EXERCISE FOR YOUR ENTIRE FAMILY

Pull down the kitchen calendar and buy a box of popcorn.

Make a big bowl of popcorn and then put the calendar in the middle of the kitchen table. Have everybody together think of every birthday they want to remember (including their own). Write the dates on the calendar. (If you don't know a person's birthday, it's a perfect excuse to have one of the children call the person right then.) On the first of every month, look at the calendar together as a family and send out birthday cards to everyone with a birthday that month.

The popcorn is just to eat!

CHAPTER 9

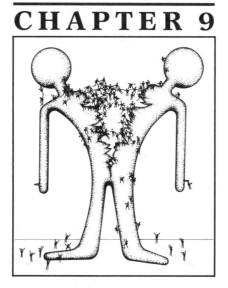

DATING AND REMARRIAGE

"I can't stand Mitch, he's such a jerk."
Doug, an eight year old, describing
his mother's boyfriend.

Sheila had been divorced for three years, and during that time had managed to help herself and her children, Doug and Patty, adjust to the changes in their family.

Doug was well-adjusted at home and had a good relationship with his father, Clark, always expressing his affection for him. Recently, however, Doug had begun to throw temper tantrums and often refused to follow Sheila's directions; he wouldn't wear the clothes she laid out, or eat his dinner, or go to bed at the agreed upon time.

The only recent change which had taken place in the family was that Sheila's relationship with her boyfriend, Mitch, had become serious and they were contemplating marriage. Mitch often joined Sheila and the children for dinner and participated in other family activities. Doug's anger at his mother appeared to be related to the new demand that he share his mother with Mitch.

When the children were alone with Mitch everyone would get along very well. Doug and Mitch would repair bicycles, watch football on T.V., and work on homework. When Sheila returned, however, Doug would become sullen and withdrawn: openly hostile toward both Sheila and Mitch.

What was so confusing to Sheila was that Doug appeared very happy that his father had recently become engaged and was planning a Christmas wedding. Doug seemed to accept Clark's fiancée, Nancy, without any reservations.

An interesting aspect of emotional responses is that they may appear unreasonable, but on very close analysis there is a logical explanation for specific feelings. The reasons or explanations, however, may remain hidden even to the person experiencing them. This is especially true among children.

Sheila felt that Doug's reaction to Mitch was inconsistent. She thought that if Doug accepted Nancy—accepted his father remarrying—he should, and would, accept her plans to marry Mitch.

Doug was indeed very upset about Mitch's intrusion into their life. Most of the time Doug lived with his mother. He had dinner with his father only every Tuesday night and visited him every other weekend. Thus, Doug did not experience Nancy, his father's fiancée, as causing so many changes. On the other hand, the presence of Mitch into Doug's custodial family was keenly felt.

Doug's reaction was normal and understandable. In reality, he was spending—and would be spending—very little time with Nancy. Another important factor was that Doug had recently learned about adult sexuality from some neighborhood friends, and he was worried that his mother might be sexually involved with Mitch. Thinking about adult sexuality was overwhelming Doug. Finally, Doug's father was making derogatory remarks about Mitch, saying, "That Mitch is a real jerk!" This became a theme for Doug to subconsciously adopt. He admired and identified with all aspects of his father, and this admiration had intensified since his father no longer lived with him.

Sheila is still seeing Mitch and they are still planning to marry. She and Mitch have a new understanding, though, that Doug will need more time and lots of their patience before he can accept Mitch as a stepfather. Doug needs to learn that he can remain loyal to his father and still like Mitch. It is also very important for Doug and Mitch to realize that they do not have to like everything about each other. Doug's anger is diminishing, as the family gives everyone permission to express concerns.

Doug has had to deal with a lot of changes. First the divorce, and now two potential remarriages. For a boy of eight, this has meant too many emotional adjustments and realignments at one time. Doug's sister Patty, however, who is only six, has adjusted much better—probably in part due to her younger age.

Time, along with understanding encouragement from both parents, is necessary if children are to accept the significant changes caused by divorce in their family. More and different concerns are thrust upon them when one or both parents begin dating, adopt a new love partner or remarry.

DATING

After a marriage ends, most people eventually build a new social life—which often includes dating. Even people who do not, for religious reasons, contemplate remarriage as long as their former spouse is alive, recognize the value of interacting with members of the opposite sex. Whether and how long to wait before dating begins, and how many different dating partners a person has, varies tremendously. Some people begin seeing other people, or one special person, before their marriage is even legally dissolved. This may not be as outrageous as it seems. Once a couple separates, they often feel "divorced," but the legal proceedings stretch out over a number of months—or in some cases even years.

Other people prefer to wait to date until the divorce is final. Even after the divorce is granted, however, it may be months, or even years, before some people feel emotionally ready or have an opportunity to date.

There will be considerable difference of opinion among divorced people about the right time and right way to begin dating. There is some danger in beginning to date too soon after a divorce. You are very vulnerable immediately following a separation, and premature serious dating can lead to getting remarried "on the rebound." Most people, however, regardless of what they believe is the "right time," will start dating when they feel emotionally open to new people and when someone becomes available to them.

Adding new people to their life at any time will have an obvious impact upon your children. There are two major factors for you to consider when thinking about how the dating phenomenon will influence your children: your own dating pattern and your attitude toward your former spouse's dating.

YOUR OWN DATING

If you begin to date, it is important that your children not feel pushed aside or replaced. It may make you feel so good to court someone or be courted that you find yourself somewhat "high." When you feel this good it is very difficult to tell your new friend or friends that you need to stay home with your children several nights a week. You may even be tempted to stay home but have your date come over to your home.

Think about how this might feel to your children. They have lost their intact family structure. Now they may feel you too will be lost, lost to a new love. Telling your children, "Larry is not trying to be your Daddy, he is just Mommy's friend," will not alleviate their feeling that you may want or need Larry more than you care for them.

By all means date Larry! Go out, get a baby sitter, have fun. Introduce Larry to your son and daughter, include them in some of your outings, even have him over to your house. But also plan time at home without Larry. Continue to do things with your children without Larry; balance your time. They need you and need "special" time alone with you—not just day-to-day "necessary" time.

This balancing act may be difficult, but it is important in helping your children feel secure. If you have primary custody of your children and only have free time every other weekend, for example, you may feel it is unfair that your former spouse can go out every night. You already have so much responsibility and now must limit your dating while your former spouse has so much freedom! You are right. It is not exactly fair, but very little about divorce can be viewed as fair. Your former spouse may feel it is unfair that you get to make the major decisions about the children and that it is unfair that he or she cannot have custody. Each of you must live with and accept the reality and limits of the divorce.

People you date can have a positive influence on your children. They may help you feel better about yourself, feel happier. If you are happy, it will help your children feel happy. By getting to know other adult men or women, your children may be exposed to new ideas and new experiences. If people you are dating genuinely like your children, they can become other supportive relationships for them.

If your children do not like the person you date, or a person you date does not like your children, this can prove to be very upsetting. Perhaps they are jealous of each other, each wanting to control you. If you are feeling these types of conflicts and pressures, talk with a professional counselor a time or two to help you sort through what is happening. Both your children and your new love interest are important to you, but you must never let any of them begin to run your life.

YOUR FORMER SPOUSE'S DATING

You are not responsible for your former spouse's dating pattern, but rather for your attitude toward his or her dating. It is critical to understand that you cannot control who or how frequently your former spouse dates. If you will accept this fact you will feel much freer and happier and it will be much easier for your children to deal with it in their own way.

You will certainly have feelings about your former spouse's caring for someone besides you. This is normal and understandable and part of the process of divorce. Be aware of these feelings and, if you can, share them with another adult. Longstanding relationships and feelings do not end or change the minute the judge signs the divorce decree. Yet, regardless of these feelings, it is very hurtful and damaging to lay them on your children.

When your former spouse begins dating or falls in love with someone else, it may stir up all sorts of feelings in you. You may experience jealousy toward the new person, anger at being replaced, sadness realizing that the marriage is over, or fear that your children will like the new person more than they like you. Perhaps you might even experience happiness or relief knowing that your former spouse is starting a new social life.

The feelings of jealousy, anger, sadness, and fear may be so intense that they strongly influence interactions between divorced parents, especially when they relate to each other about the children. Divorced parents sometimes feel the only way they have any leverage with a former spouse about dating is by limiting access to the children, or by attempting to control visitations: "You can't have Lynn to your apartment when the children are over!"

Parents confuse their children by expressing their opinions about their former spouse's new friends: "Your mother has turned into a whore, sleeping at her boyfriend's house while you are with me," or "Your father's new girlfriend thinks she is so sophisticated! I will not have her taking you shopping for school clothes," or "I forbid your mother's date to come to your baseball game, if he does I will beat him to a pulp."

When the person you loved for many years—and possibly still do—chooses someone else, it is understandable that you have a strong response. For the sake of the children, however, it is important to not let these intense feelings be seen by them. Begin to let go of feelings of attachment (love or hate) for your former spouse.

You may not want to "let go" because that will confirm that the relationship as it was between you and your former spouse no longer exists. This can be painful, for it demonstrates that both of you will not only survive your divorce but must build a new life without each other. Perhaps this is something you really do not want. Some people remain bitterly attached to their former spouse years after the divorce. They say: "I can't help it, I just can't help how I feel." If you find this happening to you, consider talking with a professional counselor or joining a divorce support group. As you master letting go you will discover that who your former spouse dates and what they do is no longer as important to you.

Your children may enjoy and gain from knowing people your former spouse dates. Allow your child this freedom, for—as with someone you date—your former spouse's new friend may be another person who really cares for your children.

SEX

One especially difficult issue for some is the question of extra-marital sex. If you are opposed to sex outside of marriage, it may be difficult to deal with the fact that your former spouse might be having sex with another with the knowledge of your children or sometimes even in the same house or apartment where they are staying.

This may reflect an important difference in values and morality between you and your former spouse—perhaps one which was a major cause of your divorce. In any case, you *cannot* use this situation as a reason to deny visitation rights. Such a denial is neither legal nor wise.

If you believe that your young children are being seriously disturbed by your former spouse's behavior, try to talk to him or her directly (and as dispassionately as possible) about it or enlist a third party to do so. Emphasize that you are not personally interested in his or her sex life, but that as parents both of you must be concerned about how each of your sexual activities affect your children. Suggest that the only issue you are concerned about is what is being communicated to the children and ask your former spouse to consider more discretion when they are around. If this does not work, *drop the subject.* Nothing that you say or do is going to change the situation.

With your children, you are free to make a clear statement of your disapproval of such activity. Once this has been done, however, only your positive example and teaching has any hope of effectively transmitting your values regarding sexual activity to your children. Continual harping on this subject with either your former spouse or your children will only leave you open to criticism for interference or ridicule for prudery.

If you are engaging in extra-marital sex yourself, remember that children are easily influenced. Be sure that your pre-adolescent child can truly handle your behavior. On the issue of your sexual behavior, discretion and common sense regarding the welfare of your children should be a major consideration.

REMARRIAGE

As if managing the emotions and relationships created when divorced parents begin to date were not complicated enough, adjustment for parents and children takes a new turn if and when either parent remarries. Remarriage seals the fate that there will be no parental reconciliation (although even children in their teens and twenties often have fantasies about reconciliation of their original family long after both parents have remarried).

Not only is the door of reality closed on reconciliation, but new people are brought into the children's lives for whom they are supposed to have, or at least begin to have, a "family" feeling. Here is another major change—just like the divorce—when children feel that they have had no control over their own family structure.

If remarriage takes place within a year or two after the divorce, children will still be in the process of adjusting. At the same time they are adjusting to the losses created by the divorce, they must also adjust to the entrance of a step-parent, sometimes bringing with him or her step-children, step-grandparents, and even step-pets.

Some of the major problem areas for remarriages are disagreements about children. These do not need to become crises between you and your new spouse, but it is important to discuss together your values and beliefs about child-rearing prior to remarriage. All family members, old and new, must realize that they are members of a remarried family and that a remarried family is *not* like an original nuclear family. An acceptance of this "differentness" may remove a lot of pressure from everyone.

If you remarry, do not expect your children to call your new spouse "Dad" or "Mom." Your children already have a father and a mother. In those rare instances where the biological parent emotionally or physically deserts the child, the child may want to call the step-parent "Mom" or "Dad" immediately. If, over time, a close parent-like relationship develops, the child may then elect to use these familial names. Allow the relationship to develop in a natural way. Many children are angry at their own mother or father for referring to the step-parent as "your Dad" or "your Mom." Be sensitive to your child's feelings, and accept his or her ongoing loyalty to the other natural parent.

Step-parents can add support and security to a single parent family, bringing to the family some additional time and energy and even money that may be very much needed. If you or your former spouse remarry, take some time to consider how this will impact your children. Have family discussions, ask the children for their input about how they would like the new family to function. Allow them to care for new family members—including members of your former spouse's new family—but don't force feelings.

If both you and your former spouse remarry your children will belong to two separate, intact, remarried families. They will still and always have, however, only one set of parents—you and your former spouse. Your original relationship will exist with your children forever.

* * *

EXERCISE 9

Bridging the New Chasms

FOR YOU

Choose one new social relationship that is causing you some discomfort. It could be your former husband's new girl friend, the son of the woman you are dating, or your former wife's new husband. Write the name of that person across the top of a piece of paper and under the name write your relationship to that person.

Form four columns across the page: "Feelings Toward (name of person)," "How They Affect Me," "How They Affect My Children," and "Possible Solutions." Decide which of the solutions you might begin to implement in the upcoming week.

(LAURA'S EXAMPLE)

KRISTINE

CHUCK'S (MY FORMER HUSBAND'S) LIVE-IN GIRLFRIEND

FEELINGS TOWARD KRISTINE	HOW THEY AFFECT ME
1. Angry	1. I loose control. I feel hot inside. I even feel sick.
2. Jealous	2. I buy new clothes to compete with her. I find myself cutting down her work. I say sarcastic things to Chuck about her.

106

HOW AFFECTS CHILDREN	POSSIBLE SOLUTIONS
1. They see me act hostile when they mention her name.	1. Begin to accept the fact that Chuck left me by choice; Kristine did not make him leave me.
They saw me slam down the phone when she called.	Meditate on forgiveness—pray for calmness.
They have heard me say sarcastic things to others about her.	Accept the fact that my girls like her.
2. They know I am not acting like myself.	2. Begin to know and like myself; (how do I do that?)
They see me as hypocritical, because I use to admire educated women.	Put energy into my own job.
They are embarrassed.	Keep quiet about Kristine.
3. Rosie (my ten year old) is beginning to ask questions about sex.	3. Begin to tell Rosie the facts of life. Explain how I feel about sex before marriage.

(COMMENT)

This short exercise was very painful for Laura because she had to admit the intensity of the anger and the jealousy she felt toward Kristine, her former husband's new girlfriend. As Laura began to see how the anger and jealousy has made her act she was shocked because she realized that Kristine and Chuck's relationship was causing her to act in a manner she did not like. She didn't want them to effect her in this way.

Laura also discovered that she had probably caused her two girls, Rosie and Lucy, embarrassment and tension. She finally realized that all of her anger and jealousy will not magically destroy Kristine, nor will it help Chuck and her to get back together. She decided to try and let go of this anger and jealousy, and move ahead with her life.

Finally, Laura was upset that Chuck and Kristine's sexual relationship was causing her oldest daughter to ask questions about sex. Laura realized that she had no desire to confront her former husband on his behavior, but she did want to make it clear to her daughters how she felt about sex outside of marriage.

At the completion of the exercise, Laura was not sure of how to begin liking herself, but she knew that was where she wanted to put her energies. The emotions she felt doing this exercise were strong, but after she completed it she felt freer, more sure of herself, and happier than she had in a long time.

The new relationships formed by your former spouse and yourself will require many additional adjustments for your children. The following exercises might be helpful to them by creating an avenue for them to express their feelings about these new relationships.

EXERCISES FOR AGES 6-8

You will need modeling clay or play dough in at least two colors.

Have your child make your new family in one color and your former spouse's family in another. (The child could make himself or herself in a third color to show that it is the same person in both families.)

After the child has "created" the family sculptures, you can talk about the differences in the two families, such as "We have four people in our family, but your Dad (or Mom) has only three." This is a good opportunity to add new people in both families—either someone you or your former spouse are seriously dating or step-parents and step-children.

If you have a doll-house or a play fort, you can encourage the child to play with the figures there, or you can merely create special "spaces" around the house for each family to "live."

EXERCISE FOR AGES 9-11

If your child is having some difficulty accepting your dating or your remarriage, ask him or her for a date. (This should be done separately for each child.) Let your child plan, within reason, what you do together. Do not make it a romantic outing, for parents should not be romantic partners, but plan a special, fun time. Go bowling, to the movies, roller skating, to the museum, hiking, etc. Have fun, enjoy being with your child.

By spending time alone with your child you are telling him or her that he or she is special! You are also communicating that as much as you like spending time with your new friend or partner, you will not forget your child. Repeat this activity on a regular basis, every month or two. It will do wonders to reduce jealousy and provide you with interesting times together.

You might also ask your child do something special for your new friend or spouse. Cook pudding together for a special dessert, draw a silly valentine, or shovel the snow off of the steps before the person comes to your home. Be sure that you work with your child (again each child separately); this should not be a *job* for the child, but a task done out of kindness for another person.

Sincerely compliment your child on his or her contribution in front of your date or new spouse. This promotes a good feeling between that person and your child.

CHAPTER 10

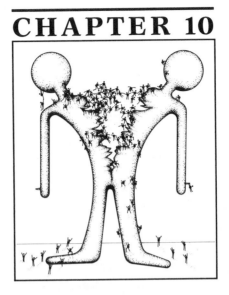

YOUR CHILD'S FUTURE

"When I grow up I'm never getting married. It's too awful to get divorced."

Stacey, an eleven year old girl.

Stacey was expressing what many children feel. They look around and see family after family divorce and wonder why. They hear their friends' horror stories concerning violence within families or witness the anger, alienation, and sadness created by their own parents' divorce. They wonder if this is the new ending to the classic romance: handsome couple meet, fall in love, marry, have children, and get divorced?

With such a vision of love, it is hardly surprising that Stacey and many other children are discounting the possibility of marriage. Your divorce may have many different impacts on your children. One major impact will be on their future—their future as adults.

As a parent, you are entrusted with the care and nurturing of your child. The "end product" of all that activity should be an adult who has the ability to live independently, the skills necessary to raise a family, the spiritual and intellectual strength to function in society, and the capacity to care and commit to others. In your role as a parent, you are supposed to eventually work yourself out of a job.

Of course, you will love your children and be interested in them all of your life, but your investment in "doing" for your children should diminish as they do more and more for themselves. What skills and emotional tasks will your child need to master to be a fulfilled adult? Will your divorce effect their mastery of these tasks?

WORKER

One primary adult role is that of worker. While adult work is not an immediate concern for pre-adolescent children, their attitudes toward work are being formed at this early age.

All healthy adult people are engaged in some form of work. Some people refer to their work as a career; this usually means that they have made an emotional commitment to their type of work. In addition to time spent on the job they invest additional time and energy learning about and pursuing aspects of their career. In past decades it has usually been men who made a commitment to a career in addition to their family, although there have always been women who have pursued careers outside the home. Women who stay home to raise the children and create a family environment often make a "career commitment" to this role. People who have careers are certainly interested in the amount of money to be earned, but they also receive emotional satisfaction from their work.

Other adults view their work as a job or an occupation. They perform the tasks needed to be successful, but do not have an emotional commitment to it. If another job that pays more but uses completely different skills becomes available, they can easily switch jobs. People who view work this way may go home feeling some anxiety or worry, but seldom invest emotional time and energy into work development. If they advance on the job—and many do—it is because they work very well. These people are often very skilled, careful workers, and get great satisfaction from doing quality work.

Jill and Karen are beauticians at a local hair salon. Jill views her work role as a career, and Karen sees it as a job. Jill attends national conferences where the latest hair styling and health trends are discussed, teaches two days a week at a vocational cosmetology school, and reads the hair styling magazines. In the future, she plans to open her own hair styling salon. Karen is a good hair stylist. She comes to work on time, and is friendly with her customers. She is not committed to cosmetology, however. Karen has two other interests she would like to pursue: full-time homemaker/mother or nurse. Karen is not married, so her first interest is not yet attainable. To realize the second, she is currently saving money to go to nursing school. If Karen realizes either goal, she may then view her work as a career because she will feel emotionally committed to her work.

Virtually everyone works partially to make the money needed to survive and prosper. In this sense, all work is partially mere "toil." All people want to see their work as providing a necessary or useful service or product, however, and want to consider what they do as having value. Most people will experience their adult work as having some qualities of a job and some of a career. The critical dimension of any adult work is for the individual engaged in the work to feel satisfied and generally happy with what he or she is doing.

Your current attitude toward your work may influence your child's view of adult options. If you feel angry or cheated at having to work outside the home or feel trapped in a particular job because of child support payments or child care responsibility or even a need to live near your children, you may be communicating this to them. When a parent is unhappy with his or her work, the message communicated to the children is "Adult work is miserable."

To help your child develop a positive future, spend the time and energy in creating an adult work role for yourself that is as personally rewarding as possible. If your children view you as generally happy with your work, it will provide them with an adult model that says "Adult work is satisfying."

Another way you can help your children develop a positive attitude toward adult work is to expose them to the many different jobs people perform. You know your children's interests and abilities. Point out those types of work you think would use these attributes and discuss them from time to time. Encourage your child to try new experiences and master new skills.

The final choice of adult work must be each child's, of course. Do not force a child into your mold, but rather encourage him or her to find the right path for himself or herself. All children need encouragement from their parents to explore many options.

From the time my son, Brian, was little, he had a fascination with the weather. He always watched the weather reports on television, kept records of the day's temperatures, and followed the paths of hurricanes and tornadoes as some children follow their favorite sports team. We often talked about careers in weather. When he went to college, however, he decided to major in pre-law because it was a career that guaranteed a good "income." While in college, though, he took courses in meteorology as electives. After graduation from college, Brian was accepted at an outstanding law school—and off he went to build a career that made lots of money. At the end of his first year of law school, Brian told me "Mom, I do not want to be a lawyer—I don't like law—I want to have a career dealing with some aspect of the weather." This made perfect sense to me. He was finally listening to himself.

In addition to my encouragement of Brian's interest in weather, perhaps my contribution to his development has been being a person who loves her own adult work. He has seen me invested and interested in my career, with financial rewards being secondary to the personal satisfaction of being engaged in social work. Brian is now pursuing a path that uses both his abilities and interests. I encouraged my son in his career, but the decision ultimately emerged from him.

Divorce can have another type of influence on the choice of adult work. If you were suddenly left with the need to have a job outside of the home, did not have the time or money necessary to develop your own career, or currently have a job that is not very satisfying but which you might have to keep "for the sake of the children," your child may vow never to be in that position. Rather than preparing for a homemaker role, your daughter may insist on thoroughly preparing herself for a "meaningful" adult role that will provide her with income. If you have a son, he may feel that before making a commitment to marry it is imperative for his prospective spouse to have career outside the home that is satisfying to her. In other words, your divorce may result in your child being very aware of—and perhaps even overly concerned with—the importance of being able to financially care for oneself and any dependent children.

Your divorce does not have to have a negative influence on your children's adult work roles. It may influence them to prepare carefully for self sufficiency; this certainly is not bad. On the other hand, it may cause them undue anxiety over financial security and self-doubt about their own abilities to function in the adult world of work. If both you and your children continue to work at accepting and understanding yourselves and the impact of the divorce on your lives, however, it will allow you to have enough energy to support your career or job development and your children to choose their own work interests.

SPOUSE

Being a husband or wife is another adult role which is far in the future for your pre-adolescent children. Yet they are forming attitudes and opinions on marriage now which will greatly affect their future actions.

It is normal and healthy to want to share your adult life with another person. To be able to take this step, one must be able to make an emotional commitment to that person. This commitment usually means you love, or deeply care for, your partner and are willing to share resources such as time, sex, money, and interests with him or her. It also implies sexual and emotional fidelity.

You were married; your marriage was a commitment to share your adult life with your former spouse. You promised to do so "... for better or worse, till death do you part." You now have experienced how a commitment made with affection and sincerity can change, shatter and end. So have your children. You may be somewhat bitter and disillusioned, perhaps feeling fearful about ever really trusting a commitment to another adult. So might your children.

After a divorce it is very normal to feel hesitant and concerned about making another "lifelong" commitment to a new partner. For some, religious beliefs or laws make remarriage impossible while their former spouse is alive unless they receive an official "annulment" of their former marriage. Yet it is quite natural to long for and desire to share your life with a new someone. Before beginning a new relationship, however, please take the time you—and your children—need to heal from the hurts and disappointments the ending of your marriage produced. During this time, try to resolve and dissolve bitter feelings toward your partner. Continuing bitterness and anger will contaminate any new relationship and will sap the positive energies needed to invest in a new partner. If you cannot bring yourself to put the past behind you for your own good, do it for your children's future ability to have successful marriages of their own.

Your children have witnessed the collapse of an adult commitment...the ending of their parent's marriage. After parental divorce, children often express doubts about ever marrying. The way you, as a parent, model your ongoing adult commitments may affect the type of partner commitments your child will make in the future. You were a partner to your child's other parent, and that commitment ended. You have other commitments, however, a commitment to your parents, your child, your friends, your job. These commitments continue after the divorce. Has your child seen you keep your word, pay your bills, do special things for family and friends? Does your child see you respect and honor the divorce decree? If you meet another adult and make an emotional commitment to him or her, your child may draw ideas about commitments from observing that relationship.

These are tangible ways you can demonstrate to your children the ability to commit. As they reach adulthood, they will be able to use these types of positive experiences to help build their own adult relationships. Your divorce may result in your child being somewhat cautious about marriage, but human beings usually want to have a close committed relationship, so most children from divorced families will grow up and marry. What you do now will foster your children's ability to fulfill that commitment.

PARENT

In addition to having a satisfying work role and a successful marriage, most adults want to be parents. Again, this is not an immediate concern to grade school children, but their parental skills are being formed even now. To parent, an adult should be able to nurture a needy, dependent baby and child. Good parenting requires one to be able to remember how it was to be a child, yet stay in the adult role of setting appropriate and safe boundaries. Your example now will do more than anything else to make your own children good parents when they grow up.

As you already know, parenting has many rewards, but it is also a lot of hard work. The relationship with your child is a lifelong commitment which cannot be dissolved. Children truly are "nondivorceable." During the divorce process, the ability to parent is often strained. You may be experiencing considerable stress trying to adjust to the many changes and losses caused by your divorce and have little time and energy left to nurture your child. Unfortunately, just when parents are at this low ebb is when their children—also suffering losses and changes—need them most.

Recognizing this need of your children may help you be more available to them. Even when you are exhausted at the end of the day, for example, just sitting together to watch T.V. or relaxing in your robes and pajamas and chatting about the day's events will be reassuring for both you and them. If your children's grandparents or aunts and uncles live close by, perhaps they can supplement your parenting by having you all over to dinner or occasionally watching your children so you can have some time to rest. Your local parish or congregation is also full of people willing to help out.

Ruth, the mother of eight year old Christine, has been emotionally victimized by her divorce for six years. Ruth cannot discuss Christine's well being or development with the child's father, George, and continues to fluctuate between depression and rage. During the six years since the divorce, Ruth has fed, clothed and schooled Christine, but she has not been able to emotionally parent. . .she has been unable to nurture.

This deprivation may well strain Christine's own ability to nurture when she grows up and has children of her own. To be able to give to another person, especially to a needy child, requires that a parent feel pretty good about himself or herself and have an inner source of empathy and giving that was built up by being emotionally cared for as a child. Christine is not getting this support from her mother, although her father, sister, grandparents, and teachers are supplying emotional nurturing. Only time will tell if it was enough for Christine to be able to be a nurturing parent herself.

The most important thing you can do to help your child grow up with the ability to parent is to put the energy and effort into parenting your own child now.

FRIEND AND CITIZEN

Family and work roles usually make up the emotional center of one's life. There are, however, many other roles that adults are required to fulfill. Now, too, is the time when your children are forming their ideas regarding friendship and citizenship. Many of these roles can be very enriching, fulfilling, and supportive. In all of the events of daily life, you interact with others and are performing the role of friend, consumer, neighbor, volunteer and citizen. It is in these roles that we go beyond our own narrow interests and concerns and exhibit the spirit of service, sharing and giving.

Interaction with people outside of the home and work help you feel connected to the community and the world. This type of connectedness helps people get through times of stress. People who have an established network of friends and acquaintances through church or synagogue and community involvement usually adjust faster to divorce and other losses. Here again, it is up to you to provide the role model for your children.

Barbara was devastated when her husband announced he wanted a divorce and left her with three children. For the past fifteen years Barbara and her former husband had lived in the same community. During those years, she had established many friends and acquaintances. The friendships were established through many differing connections: work friends, friends made through years of active church membership, neighborhood friends, friends from her childhood, and friends from an exercise class. Although her divorce was very painful, Barbara had the help and support of many other people. While many divorced people find that they lose contact with friends that they had as a couple with their former spouses, Barbara worked very hard to insure that this did not happen to her. She took an apartment in her old community, stayed a member of her church, even kept up her exercise class. She managed to keep most of her friends, and they supported her in her troubles. All of this communicated to her children the nature of adult friendship.

Tom had always been interested in politics and for a time was involved in a local municipal campaign for the mayoral election. When he and his wife divorced, Tom experienced many lonely evenings—even though he had two children. At the suggestion of a friend, Tom went to the local office of a major political party and began working as a volunteer for fifteen hours a month. It was the year of a presidential campaign, so there was a lot for Tom to do. In addition to having something to occupy his spare time, Tom met some interesting new friends, went to political rallies, and realized satisfaction in making a contribution to a cause which was important to him. Tom's children saw how this involvement was helpful to him and it taught them a valuable lesson about the benefits of civic involvement.

Tom and Barbara are examples of how people have utilized their connectedness and interests in the world outside of work and family to help them adjust to divorce. In both of these cases, the interests or friendships were established as a natural part of their adult life. By their own example, Barbara and Tom were helping their children develop the skills necessary to form adult networks.

Encourage your children to be involved in activities and friendships. Allow over-nights, birthday parties, swim lessons, drum lessons, and church camp. Support their participation in programs that help others, such as walk-a-thons, food drives and visiting the elderly. These experiences will give your children exposure to outside institutions such as the church or synagogue and the "Y" or the public parks. From this exposure they will begin to view the world as a place where one can gain support and help others. Social interactions will help your children develop the skills to make and keep friends and be involved in their community when they are adults.

A word of caution is in order: although you should allow your children to be engaged in activities outside of the home, do *not* "over-enroll" your child. Some divorced parents have their children in some activity every afternoon of the week and on sports teams on the weekends. This is *too much* structured activity. Children also need time to just "be."

Your divorce does not need to hamper your children's ability to have satisfying friendships and community involvement. As with all preparation needed for adult roles, their parents' ability to emotionally recover from the divorce is a most critical factor in children's development. As you emotionally heal yourself, you will be able to help your children engage in activities outside of the home.

EXERCISE 10
Imagining Your Child's Future

FOR YOU

Write on a piece of paper these three columns: "How I Feel," "What I Am Communicating To My Children," and "What I Can Do About It." In the center of the

116

paper under these headings write these four adult roles: "Worker," "Spouse," "Parent," and "Friend and Citizen." Under each category, list how your current attitudes and actions are affecting your child's preparation for their adult roles. Decide which of your solutions you can initiate in the next week.

(GERRY'S EXAMPLE)

HOW I FEEL	WHAT AM I COMMUNICATING	WHAT CAN I DO
	WORKER	
1. Bored	a. Being an accountant is a boring profession.	a. Ask my boss for a new assignment.
		b. Take some courses in new accounting methods.
2. Angry at not having the freedom to become a writer.	a. I don't have confidence in my own writing ability.	a. Send the short-story I have been working on into a magazine.
	SPOUSE	
1. Gunshy. I make jokes about marriage.	a. Marriage is a very risky and difficult business.	a. Talk to my parents and others who have a good marriage. Take the children along.
	b. Being single is better.	b. Read some good books on marriage.
	PARENT	
1. Upset at only seeing the kids every other week.	a. Maybe I don't enjoy seeing them.	a. Get a better attitude during their visits.
	b. Their mother is to blame.	b. Ask my former spouse to change the visitation agreement.
2. Really pleased to be a father.	a. My children feel loved.	a. Keep up the good work!
	FRIEND AND CITIZEN	
1. Sorry I've lost contact with my male friends.	a. You lose your friends when you get divorced.	a. Have a poker party with my friends while the kids are over.
	b. Friends aren't very important.	b. Talk to the kids about their friends.
2. Disgusted with politicians.	a. All politicians are crooked.	a. Take the kids with me when I vote.

(COMMENT)

Gerry, a divorced father who does not have custody, did this exercise and realized how negative he was being with his children. He decided that he really did not want to communicate this negativity to them and resolved to do things with them that would present a more positive image of the major adult roles.

On his work, Gerry resolved to do something to get out of his present situation. He realized that while he was not financially free to leave his accounting job, he could try to make his present job more interesting. He also resolved to pursue his interest in writing, even if it was only as a freelance writer.

Gerry felt very bitter about his divorce, and this was reflected in his attitude toward marriage. This exercise helped him realize that he might be transferring this attitude to his three children.

Although he realized that he was communicating that he was upset with the current visitation arrangements, Gerry was certain that his children felt loved. He resolved to try to change the visitation agreement, but meanwhile he gave himself praise for his parenting. (It is important to recognize those things you are doing well!)

Finally, Gerry realized that he was losing contact with his male friends and that this was giving the wrong message to his children. He also decided that his comments on politicians—even though they were done half in jest—might be forming negative attitudes in his children which he really did not want them to have.

The two following exercises will enable you to aid your children in thinking about their own futures as adults.

EXERCISE FOR AGES 6-8

You will need a large piece of paper for each of you, scissors, school glue, crayons, and several old magazines. If you have more than one child, this exercise can be done with all of the children together; a lot of talking can go on while everyone cuts and pastes. Sit on the floor or at the kitchen table. At the top of each sheet of paper write "My Future Life." Now each of you look through the magazines and cut out pictures of anything you would like to have in your future. Let your imaginations run free—a cruise, a modern new apartment, a quiet back yard, Robert Redford, a fancy bicycle—include what ever seems something you would like, regardless of how impossible this may appear. Now paste your pictures on your sheet of paper in any pattern or style. When you have your pictures finished, place them on the refrigerator or kitchen wall for a week or two. Just looking at your wishes and fantasies will give you a good feeling.

Doing this exercise with your child can be a fun "together" time. Also, creating the collage will help your child understand that there are many possibilities for the future for both of you. Your child can begin to realize that your divorce does not have to hinder that future.

As you work with your child the topic of divorce may never come up, which is fine. Do not push a discussion of your divorce; instead encourage your minds to explore the future together.

EXERCISE FOR AGES 9-11

You will need paper, a pen and an old jar or container with a secure top.

Tell your child that you are going to create a "time capsule." Divide the paper into four columns. Have the child title the columns:

1. "In high school I hope to. . ."
2. "Jobs that sound interesting to me are. . ."
3. "Places I might like to live are. . ."
4. "When I have grown up, people in my family might include. . ."

Ask your child to write at least four responses under each heading. Some children may have difficulty getting started. They may need some help in freeing up their minds to explore a variety of possibilities. If your child is stuck, perhaps you can suggest a response such as "In high school, I wanted to have some good friends. Is this something you hope for too?"

Children need to learn that expressing hopes and dreams is not foolish, for it is from these dreams that their future will be built.

When the child is finished, have him or her put the paper into the container and close the top. Write on the container: "TIME CAPSULE—DO NOT OPEN UNTIL (date of child's 16th birthday). Then spend some time together finding a good "hiding place."

You may find that the child wants to reopen the capsule to change or add to the list or to show it to a friend or even your former spouse. Or he or she might want to open it every birthday in order to update it. All of these options are fine! Eventually the child will forget about the capsule, and on his or her 16th birthday, it will be a great source of merriment and insight for him or her.

CONCLUSION

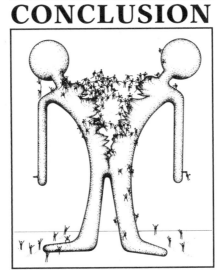

THE ONGOING NATURE OF DIVORCE

"Mom, when is the divorce going to be over?"

Ethan, a six year old boy.

Do not think that as you finish this book you are through helping your child deal with your divorce. That process will take a lifetime. Some people are still grappling with their parents' divorce when they themselves reach their 40's.

Children need to communicate over and over about their parents' divorce. There will be critical periods in your child's life when your divorce may again become a concern and interest. One such time is when the child is between the ages of eleven and thirteen. At this time a child is just beginning to work on establishing an independent identity. The question of "Who am I?" suddenly becomes very important. To know "Who I am," your child needs to know who each parent is: "I am my parent's child."

At this age, it is not uncommon for a child to begin to voice a desire to live with the non-custodial parent. This happens even in families where children have a very good relationship with their custodial parent. This desire to live with the other parent may be motivated by an inner desire to "really know" that other parent. Deciding whether custody should be changed is a very complex process and is well beyond the scope of this book. If your child expresses this desire it probably would be wise to explore your child's wish with a professional counselor.

Do *not* panic, overreact, or become angry. On the other hand, you also should not give immediate consent to the transfer of custody. Explore your child's expressed desire over a period of time with someone outside the family before a final decision is made.

Another critical period appears to be when a child is between the ages of fifteen to seventeen. At this age the adolescent is beginning to have experiences with love and sexuality. This may raise questions about the love and sexuality of his or her parents. "How did you meet Dad?" or "How could you sleep with another woman when you were still legally married to Mom?" are some examples of the questions children may ask . . .or want to know but are afraid to ask. It is important not to discount or avoid your children's questions, they are nearing adulthood and want honest, adult answers.

Other times your children may need to process the divorce are when they are contemplating marriage or having their own children, when you remarry or move far away, or upon the occasion of a family tragedy—especially the death of one of the parents. All of these events are times of change and may trigger some unresolved emotions or questions related to the losses of the childhood family.

You, too, may be especially vulnerable in times of transition. Do not avoid these feelings or questions. Allow yourself and your children to continue the lifelong healing, acceptance, understanding process.

Here are some final "tips" that may be useful to you and your children in successfully navigating the process that takes your from the pre-divorce family to your current family and into the future.

1. Take care of yourself . . . physically, emotionally, and spiritually.

Every aspect of your child's well-being depends on you being healthy. When the shock of divorce first descends, you may feel very tired. Get the rest you need; go to bed earlier than usual, if necessary. Eat well balanced meals, and do not overconsume alcohol or coffee. If your tiredness persists see your doctor.

For your emotional health talk to others. You know how crucial it is to share your anger, worry, frustration, sadness, and successes with an understanding friend. Also, try to begin helping someone else; see if you too can listen. Finally, listen to your inner self . . .your spirit. God's grace is always there when we need it. If you find your church or synagogue a place where you sense peace and develop insights, continue to draw upon this support. The disillusionment of the divorce may have triggered a questioning of your former beliefs. If you reject them, both you and your children will be experiencing an additional loss . . .the loss of a spiritual base at a time when it is most needed.

All people need to sense a connectedness to their spirit, and this connectedness may not have anything to do do with a formal religion. It has to do with an "inner knowing." There are many avenues to rebuild or to discover your spiritual dimension: talking with an understanding member of the clergy, walking in the quiet woods, playing the piano, reading, meditating, writing, or taking care of an infant or elderly person are examples of how some people have found their spiritual selves. By listening to your inner self you will discover a strength that can help you transcend this period of upheaval.

2. Let go of intense anger toward your former spouse (your child's other parent) for the hurt that he or she caused.

To help your child, the most important thing you can do—next to taking care of yourself—is to begin to dissipate the anger toward your former spouse for all of the wrongs that you feel were perpetrated against you. It may be difficult, if not impossible, to take this step, but even the effort is helpful. This does not mean you should never have felt anger toward your former spouse. It is very healthy to feel and express anger when someone has hurt you. If the anger remains intense, long after the hurtful incidents have occurred, however, it will definitely begin to interfere with your current, ongoing functioning.

If you are not yet ready to give up your hate, then please try to set this as future goal. If you do remain hateful, your children will suffer more than anyone else.

3. Try to build a co-parenting relationship with your former spouse.

The children who fare the best after parental divorce are those whose parents can discuss and share matters that pertain to the children. This in no way implies that the divorced parents need to be best friends or chat about their personal lives. It means that both spouses are entitled to know pertinent information about their children and participate in the important decisions affecting them.

Sharing report cards is a good start, but do not stop there. Share concerns about your child's development. Tell each other about your child's fears and hopes. Do not wait for the "other" parent to build this type of communication; take the initiative yourself.

Another word of caution: do not use the concept of "co-parenting" to try to get closer to your former spouse for romantic or other personal interests. This is using your children. A co-parenting relationship should be just what the term implies; two parents who care very much about their child sharing ideas and tasks to help in successfully raising the child.

4. Provide and encourage alternative sources of support for your child.

Children need and deserve all the love and affection that they can get. During the divorce process there may be many times when your energy and time will be consumed by the many tasks and emotions you are facing. If your child has additional sources of love and affection, he or she can draw upon these during the times you are feeling drained.

Grandparents can be a wonderful source of support. If they are the patient kind, grandparents will not mind taking your children on long outings and then stopping for ice cream. Let your parents—or your former spouse's parents—help nurture your child. Aunts, uncles, cousins and adult friends are all additional possibilities for support for your children. Pets are also a source of love which children treasure. A family dog or cat does not talk back or take away toys and will often sit with children while they watch the most boring T.V. cartoon.

5. Encourage, but do not force, your child to express feelings.

There are children who will not, or cannot, express their feelings. Some children simply cannot label their feelings—they know they feel something but they don't know what to call it. Other children do not want to tell anyone their feelings, they want to protect their private emotions. Still other children have repressed their feelings about the divorce to such an extent that they really believe that they have no feelings about it.

Of course, everyone involved in a divorce has some feelings about it. All children whose parents divorce have feelings about the divorce. If your child refuses to share his or her feelings do not push, pry, or intrude; but do continue to be open yourself. Occasionally, share what you think your child, or any child, might be feeling in this situation, but allow your child the freedom not to comment.

Children sometimes can be open about divorce feelings with someone other than their parents. This other person might be a special friend, a brother or sister, a teacher, or counselor. Do not take it as a personal slight if your child talks more easily to another about the divorce. Understand that if your child does not share feelings with you it may be because he or she is trying to protect you or feels uncomfortable in sharing positive feelings about the other parent. Be happy that your child can talk to someone; in time your child may be able to share with you.

6. Expect your child to have some feelings that are different than yours.

If your child does share his or her feelings with you, remember that these feelings may not be at all similar to yours. Your child may think that your former spouse is very nice and express a desire to spend more time with that parent. If you have a bad look on your face when you hear these feelings expressed, or try to talk your child out of feeling a certain way, he or she will eventually get the message, "You can have feelings as long as they are exactly what I want you to have." When both parents send this message, children are put into a position in which they can never be honest. Try very hard not to convey this message your child; permit your child to view the divorce from his or her own perspective.

7. Do things with your child.

During the process of divorce you may often feel overwhelmed with things to do. It may seem like that there is little time left to do fun, extra activities with your child. It is important, however, to try and include space for your child. Perhaps on a Sunday afternoon you can stop for ice cream, or after dinner you can take a fifteen minute bike ride. This type of attention will demonstrate to your children that despite the divorce they are going to continue to be cared for. It will help your children feel secure.

8. Do thing with people other than your child.

You are interested in your child and are putting time and energy into helping him or her adjust to the divorce. This is necessary and commendable. But be careful not to let your child become the only person or interest in your life. You need grown up, adult friends, too, and you need to spend some time doing adult activities. . .time without your child.

If you have other interests and friends it will help your child's development. Your child will see you enjoying the outside world, and it will give him or her the message that it is possible to be a happy adult.

9. Encourage your child to develop and master his or her emerging abilities.

During the years your child is in grammar school, he or she will begin to want to "try out" some new interests and develop new ideas and skills. If—because of parental divorce—the child does not have the energy, encouragement or resources to invest in the development of these interests and skills, they may lie dormant and unused all of his or her life. A valuable growth period will be missed.

Do not push your child into too many activities or "over schedule" your child's life. Rather be in tune with your child and encourage him or her to build a base of experiences and skills that will be the beginning of a self-confident adult. Being on a ball team and learning to practice hard, to win, and to lose; learning to pitch a tent and cook a dinner over a camp fire; going on the bus to the dentist are examples of confidence-building experiences that may enrich a child's development.

10. If either you—or your child—are having difficulties, consider seeking professional help.

Your divorce may be such a stressful process that—as hard as you may try to get your life functioning again—you may keep running into emotional, social, or financial problems. If you or your child continue to feel intense bitterness, sadness, or helplessness, perhaps a professional counselor could be helpful. Social workers and psychologists that work with divorcing families often know of resources available in your community. Just becoming linked with the right support (money, legal, child care, job search, housing, Big Brother/Sister, health services, and so on) may lift a big load off of your shoulders.

After all, neither you nor your child have never gone through what you are going through now. How could you be expected to know what help is available? A professional counselor can also help you and your child explore the troublesome aspects of your divorce. Many people feel more comfortable discussing very private feelings and events with a stranger who is a professional. The professional relationship is confidential and a counselor will be listening and thinking only of your well-being.

Perhaps you believe that you cannot afford professional help. Do not let that stop you! Some counselors charge a on sliding scale (the fees are fixed on the basis of your ability to pay), and many religious agencies and mental health agencies provide free counseling or will put you in contact with a counselor you can afford. If you feel that you would like to talk with such a professional counselor, get out your yellow pages and look under "Family Counseling," "Social Workers," or "Psychologists." Make a call or two to find out what is available.

Another alternative is to join a support group. There are a variety of such groups organized by churches or synagogues, schools and social agencies. There are support groups for the recently divorced, for those without partners for whatever reasons, and for single parents. Such support groups allow you to share what you are going through with others who are experiencing or have been through the same things. You might find you even want to continue in such a group to help other people deal with the problems of divorce and single parenting.

Finally, use the exercises in this book whenever you think that they will be helpful to you or your child. Perhaps you may find some of them useful again in two or three years, when a younger child is at an age to engage in the older exercises or when one of your school age children has additional concerns or questions about the divorce.

* * *

Being a parent is a lifelong commitment which will bring you joy, anger, frustration, success, fun, worry, heartbreak and satisfaction. The effort you have made to help your children accept and understand your divorce is just one of the many, many responsibilities of parenthood.

The fact that you are willing to make the special efforts involved in being a divorced parent is a large step toward fulfilling your commitment to your children.

ALSO OF INTEREST

TEENS ARE NONDIVORCEABLE by Sara Bonkowski. This is the companion volume to *Kids Are Nondivorceable*, specifically written for parents with teenage children 12-18 years old. 160 pages, $7.95.

LIVES UPSIDE DOWN: SURVIVING DIVORCE by James Flosi. Uses actual stories of divorcing people and their children to illustrate the four "stages" that most divorces go through. 96 pages, $5.95.

ANNULMENT: A STEP BY GUIDE FOR DIVORCED CATHOLICS by Ronald T. Smith. This helpful, up-to-date guide provides practical information about each of the steps involved in the annulment process, along with helpful insights into healing and moving forward with one's personal and spiritual life. 128 pages, $8.95.

DIVORCE AND BEYOND by James Greteman and Leon Haverkamp. This support-group program for newly divorced persons focuses on the "mourning period" of the divorce process and concentrates mainly in the divorced persons themselves, rather than on their role as parents. Participant's Book, 132 pages, $4.95; Facilitator's Manual, 80 pages, $4.95.

TO TRUST AGAIN by William Urbine. A complete, self-contained program for marriage preparation for couples in which one or both parties have been involved in a previous marriage which ended through death or divorce. Couple's Workbook, 48 pages, $4.95; Leader's Guide, 48 pages, $9.95; Remarriage Inventory, 32 pages, $4.95.

MEDITATIONS (WITH SCRIPTURE) FOR BUSY MOMS by Patricia Robertson. Insightful, down-to-earth reflections for each day of the year paired with surprising and illuminating quotes from the Bible. 368 pages, $8.95.

MEDITATIONS (WITH SCRIPTURE) FOR BUSY DADS by Patrick T. Reardon. A companion to the Moms book just for Dads. 368 pages, $8.95.

Available at bookstores or by calling 800-397-2282.